Investing in Art
In the Digital Age
By RL Foster

Innovative Books
Denver, Colorado

Innovative Books
2018

Investing in Art in the Digital Age
By RL Foster

Copyright ©2018 by RL Foster

All rights reserved. No part of this book may be reproduced or transmitted in any form or by any means, electronic or mechanical, including photocopying, or by an information storage and retrieval system without permission in writing from the publisher.

Innovative Books
P.O. Box 221734
Denver, Colorado 80222

info@innovativebooks.net

ISBN 9781983974434

Contents

Introduction 1
Art collecting versus art investing.......... 5
Why invest in art? 7
Why not invest in art? 10
Evaluating art 14
Appraisals and authentications 22
Buying art 28
Selling art 36
Auctions..........41
Insurance 46
Art and estate planning 50
Art and law 53
Art consultants and advisers 58
Other art investments..........63
How the internet has changed the art market 67
Speculating in art: the return of the patron 71
Final words: buyer beware..........75

Appendixes

Art auction terms 80
Informative websites 83

Introduction

The last twenty-five years of my life has been dominated by the art business. I came out of a media background as a writer and a publisher, and gravitated into the field of arts. Through this media experience, I joined a major Denver gallery as their marketing director and was drafted as the gallery appraiser. I ultimately opened my own gallery and continued to pursue art appraising.

Although I have always had the ability to discern good art, I have little natural painting ability, and have been more interested in art history and the economic side of art. The one conclusion that my study has shown me is that the business of art has always been challenging. From the early Renaissance, artists have struggled to support themselves with their art. The popular legend that Vincent Van Gogh only sold one painting in his life is not far from the truth. Van Gogh's contemporary Henri Toulouse-Lautrec constantly complained that his aristocratic family didn't provide him with enough money for he found it difficult to live on his art sales. At the height of his career, American realist pioneer Robert Henri showed 50 of his paintings at a Chicago exhibition without a single sale. Few artists have personalities well fitted for the kind of self-promotion that gurantees success. Pablo Picasso, Salvador Dali and Andy Warhol were a few of the rare exceptions.

Galleries have not had it any easier. In the mid-nineteenth century, galleries first appeared. Like the artists they represented, galleries have struggled to attain profitability. The literature mentions some of the important galleries associated with the success of some historical artists, but history rarely mentions the many galleries that failed. The point is that art has always been a difficult business for those who make it; those who sell it and those who invest in it.

Newspaper stories detailing recent auction sales of paintings selling for $100 million and more distorts the very difficult reality of realizing profits as an art investor. After examining these multi-million dollar sales, we often discover the actual rate of return for even these pieces was not much greater than other financial investments. There are a few collectors who have succeeded financially as art investors, but for the great majority of collectors this is not the case.

This book is directed primarily to the collector who purchases art for the sake of investment. In actuality, the number of true art investors in American is relatively small and most of them are fairly knowledgeable and probably have little need for this book.

The reader who may benefit most from this book is the new art collector who is motivated by aesthetic considerations as well as financial ones. In a market in which there is no true blue book of prices and where the value of the commodity is greatly determined by subjective factors, it is very easy to overpay for art. So even when collectors are not particularly motivated to make profits from their art purchases, most want to build their collection in the a cost efficient manner.

There are many factors that determine the transaction price for art. Where you buy and where you sell art has a significant influence on the selling price. For instance, the prices that a living artist realizes for his or her work can be considerably higher in a gallery then you would find at an auction. I recently attended an auction where a very nice piece from a popular American realist sold for $6,000. The same piece in his major gallery would have sold for $25,000. The artist has the potential to be historically significant, but regardless of the future possibilities, one would certainly prefer a basis of $6,000 instead of the $25,000.

I have suggested to collectors that they may not always make money when they purchase a piece of art, but they certainly may be able to save money with intelligent buying and selling decisions. When I operated my gallery, I was struck by the reality that the nicest people always paid the highest price for art. I tried to reward my best collectors by providing unrequested discounts and at the same time not to allow the "grinders" to negotiate huge discounts. Perhaps that explains my departure from the gallery business.

Where you sell art is as important as where you buy the art. Collectors purchase the majority of their art from galleries (although this is declining), while the majority of their sales take place at auctions. The choice of auction has huge effect on the final price. A piece that is sold at a regional auction house might bring double at a major auction house. The time and the type of auction also exercises a major influence on art sale prices.

A major theme of this book is how the internet has changed the art business. When I review pre-internet books in my library, I am amazed how much of the content has become outdated. For the 200 years before the internet, much of the art business has remained the same. The internet has changed all of that with the most prominent development — the decline of the commercial gallery.

With the development of web technology, there has been an expansion of new outlets to buy and sell art. Online auctions have flourished, and regional auction houses now use the internet to greatly expand their base of buyers and sellers. There are hundreds of online galleries — many of them an remnants of brick and mortar galleries that have closed. Perhaps the most dramatic change is the number of artists who now promote and market their own pieces. For the collector who wants to deal directly with the artist, the internet has made that an easy reality.

In many ways the internet has tightened profit opportunities in art dealing. This is true for both the professional broker as well as the private collector-investor. Still, opportunities exist, but the collector has to be much more savvy than pre-internet collectors. This book does not make any absolute claims of getting rich in the art market, but it does provide the kind of information that is necessary for making the right decisions. I cannot guarantee you will make money in the art business, but it will help you save money.

DISCLAIMER

I should note that I am neither an attorney or accountant so the reader should consult an attorney and/or accountant for matters of estate management and taxation. Although the tax code for art has been fairly stable over the past couple of decades, there are no assurances that political winds will not change, and the law with it. You can never have enough information, and this particularly true of the art market.

Art collecting versus art investing

Art investing is often confused with art collecting. All art investors are art collectors, but not all art collectors are investors. An art investor acquires art primarily for the purpose of reselling the work in the future for profit. Art investors usually acquire art they find to be visually appealing, but that is not their primary motivation. An art investor may never sell the work, but that was not the original intention. An art collector acquires art for the enjoyment of its aesthetic and intellectual pleasure. The art collector may eventually sell a work, but that was not the original intention.

An art investor may also be confused with a dealer. Both the investor and the dealer intend to sell their acquired art, but the time frame for each is quite different. The art investor thinks in terms of years, even decades while the art dealer's frame of reference is much shorter. The art dealer hopes to turn over his art in a very short time, sometimes in days or weeks. The art investor normally purchases the art from some intermediary such as a dealer or an auction, whereas the art dealer normally deals directly with owners of art. Dealers usually generate most of their income from their art whereas an investor does not.

An art speculator purchases the art for much for the same reasons as the art investor. The fundamental difference is the kind of art each purchases. The investor purchases investment grade art, while the speculator purchases art that is anticipated to become investment grade art. Thus, speculators will be much more likely to purchase contemporary art as opposed to the investors, who seek art from artists who have established reputations with secondary art market history.

Both the art collector and the art investor may act as an art patron in which case the motivation of the individual is also to support the artist. In this case, the collector is usually fond of the artist and finds the artwork appealing. An art patron may also believe in the potential investment value of the art.

Investment grade art is always high-priced so art investors are usually affluent. An art collector can purchase art for virtually any amount. Even people with very moderate incomes can be collectors. Dealers require capital to finance their inventory. Often, dealer's inventories are funded by others, including art investors who are clients of the dealer. Depending on the art which they collect, an art collector may be very affluent or not.

An art speculator requires some affluence, because even speculative art can be costly and since the goal is long term investment, no income will be generated in the short term.

It has been estimated that only one in fifty adults ever purchases an original piece of art. Perhaps, half of these people may be called "collectors." Even though art collecting is an activity of relatively few people, American art collectors could be numbered in the hundreds of thousands whereas the number of true art investors is probably in the hundreds. How many people can afford to buy a painting for a million dollars and put it in a vault for forty years?

Why invest in art?

In today's financial reality where banks are paying less than 1% on deposits, investors are seeking other investment opportunities that can yield higher rates of return. One of those opportunities is to invest in art. Indeed, art offers distinctive investment potential, but the investor should understand the real challenges of making money in art.

When we invest in anything, we are attempting to maximize our return on that investment, given some level of acceptable risk. All financial investments involve a balance between return and risk. Investing in art is no different. We have to ask: "What is the expected rate of return, and what are the risks?"

There are four major financial reasons to invest in art. The primary reason is to diversify the investor's portfolio and thereby reducing its risk. Secondly, a savvy art collector can realize a rate of return that exceeds other more conservative investment vehicles. Thirdly art provides an inflation hedge. Lastly, for some investors, investing in art can offer some tax advantages.

Although not necessarily a financial reason, art investing offers non-pecuniary pleasures that are unique to collecting art. These pleasures include the aesthetic and decorative pleasure of art and the social opportunities related to art collecting.

Rate of return

Calculating a rate of return on art investment is difficult. The difficulty lies in devising a performance index that accurately reflects the movement in art prices. The rate of return for all art is impossible to determine because a generic art bundle cannot be defined. I am considering only what I call investment grade art. This is the art that is offered by the major auction houses such as Christie's and

Sotheby's — not the art you might find in a downtown gallery. Admittedly, this criterion is not precise, but is the most accurate and valuable identifier.

There have been several indexes created to measure the changes in art prices. One the most respected indexes of investment grade art is the Mei Moses All-Art Index. The index was developed by two New York University professors, and is often quoted as the most reliable in describing art price fluctuations. This index indicates that art prices have almost matched the performance of stocks, and over some periods, the rate of return on art has beaten the stock market. This would put the annualized rate of return somewhere close to 6%.

Other estimates for price growth in art have not been so optimistic. In fact, some estimates place the rate of return near zero. A study directed by Luc Renneboog of Netherlands, Tilburg University estimates the rate of growth from 1970 to 1997 to be around 4%. We can speculate that the long-term rate of return for investment grade art is somewhere between 2% and 6% with 4% probably a fairly decent estimate depending on the art bundle.

In today's economy where certificates of deposit are yielding close to 0%, a 4% yield on fine art would appear attractive.

Asset diversification

It is a fundamental premise of financial management that asset diversification can reduce overall risk of a portfolio of assets. Adding new financial assets to any portfolio should serve to reduce risk, especially if the performance of the new asset does not correlate directly with the performance of other assets in the portfolio. Although price swings of stocks and fine art are often paralleled, they are not always perfectly in sync. Stock prices usually reflect the current level of economic activity whereas art is not as directly impacted.

Art prices are primarily a factor of supply and demand. Although there is more art being produced on this planet than ever before, the supply of investment grade art continues to decline.

Individuals not only have to compete with other collector-investors, but also from institutional buyers such as museums. There is little doubt that the long-term prospect for art is extremely positive. Like other types of real property assets, art can serve as inflation hedge

Inflation hedge

Real property can provide a hedge against inflation. Whereas inflation can eat into the value of monetary based assets such as bonds and certificates of deposits. Like real estate, coins, and gold, art is real property. Although the supply of art continues to grow, the demand for investment grade art is growing even faster. Renoir and Picasso have long stopped painting. Periods of hyper inflation, have always seen huge increases in the prices of investment grade fine art.

Current economic policy favoring deficits will eventually lead to inflation and an expanding national debt. In order to reduce the debt, one monetary tactic would be to inflate the currency, and such actions have driven economies into hyperinflation. Although inflation has been relatively stable for the last decade, there are little assurances this will continue. Art as an inflation hedge could become a very significant future advantage.

Tax advantages

Long term capital gains are taxed at lower rates than ordinary income. Although the long term capital gains for collectibles such as art are taxed at a higher rate (28%) than other financial assets (20%), the rate is still less than income tax rates for the wealthiest individuals. A portfolio in art offers the possibility of other tax advantages if the owner donates the art to qualifying charities, especially museums. In the same vein, fine art assets can play a significant role in an individual's estate planning.

The new tax law has included the elimination of some deductions for philanthropic donations, which also diminishes the value of art as a tax shelter. In this polarized political environment, it is certainly conceivable that current policy could be reversed with future administrations.

Joy of collecting

There are other opportunities that can be derived from art investing — the joy of collecting and displaying an art collection. One might argue if you are going to collect art, you might as well pursue the collecting seriously with an aim of ultimately making a profit from the activity. But there is a danger of developing the mind-set of a collector if you are attempting financial gain. Investors make money in art when they sell to collectors — not the reverse.

Summary

So why invest in art? Probably the most compelling reason is the reduction of portfolio risk by diversification and as an inflation hedge. Although a 4-6% return on investment, surpasses money-based assets, it falls behind stocks and precious metals. However, art prices are greatly determined by supply and demand. The supply of investment grade art is diminishing as contemporary artists gravitate to electronic art mediums. Paint on canvas for the current generation of artists is passé and new electronic forms of art-making add nothing to inventory of marketable art. This trend may not be immediately felt on the art market, but could have a tremendous effect in twenty or thirty years. Investing in art is always a long term proposition.

By combining the possible financial gains from investing in art with the emotional pleasure of owning and displaying the art, then art investment can be "profitable."

Why not invest in art?

There are dozens of articles on the internet praising the potential of art as an investment option, but the prudent investor should not overlook the many reasons not to invest in art.

Rate of Return

The expected rate of return that one might expect from a portfolio of investment grade art will be around 4%. Compared to interest-bearing investments, this is not poor return, but compared to the long-term rate of return for stocks at 6%, the return is inferior, especially when you consider the heightened risks that are associated with investing in art.

The long-term prospects for fine art are positive, but this time frame is in decades not years.

Risk

The volatility of art prices are similar to those of equities, and is probably a bit higher. Although the art of the very highest echelon of artists, such as Van Gogh, Klimt and Picasso hold their value, prices of secondary investment artists are much more volatile. And even major artists will have art that tumbles at times at auction

Besides financial risks, art is also subject to fraud risks. We don't have to look far to see such risks in other financial markets that are supposedly regulated. The art market is basically an unregulated market, and it has its share of schemers.

The value of art is purely subjective. I have been asked many times why a particular artist or piece of art is valued as it is. My answer, "Art is what people will pay for it."

The value of art is subject to persuasive manipulation by its sellers. Appraisals, although can be helpful, can also be deceptive. As an art appraiser, I have had collectors show me appraisals for artwork that is significantly overvalued. Recently, a collector wanted me to reappraise a Norman Rockwell print, which he had an appraisal stating the print was worth $70,000 in 1970. He was optimistic a new appraisal would push that price even higher. He was not too pleased to receive my appraisal of $750.

Even dealers who are honest can sell work that is not what it is presented to be. Spectacular art forgeries have been perpetrated against some very knowledgeable art professionals including the major auction houses. When a collector buys a piece from a dealer, he or she assumes the piece is genuine. If it is not, the buyer has little recourse unless he can show that the seller was aware that it was not genuine. A million dollar painting that is discovered to be a forgery is basically a million dollar loss, and there is no insurance that can protect the buyer from this possibility.

Transaction costs

One of the greatest obstacles in making money in art is the high transaction costs. The transaction cost for purchasing stock can be under 1% whereas the transaction costs for art may be 30% with buyer auction commissions of 20% and more. On very expensive acquisitions, this may be reduced, but it will always be significant compared to the transaction costs of other financial assets.

If the rate of return for fine art is about 4%, that means the investor will need to hold the painting for about five years before its value will just cover the transaction costs.

When an investor is working with a dealer, there is always an implied transaction costs. The dealer's selling price obviously exceeds his acquisition cost. Occasionally, there are great "deals," but when someone says, "I have a great deal for you," your risk has just escalated.

Insurance and handling

Displaying your art collection provides pleasure to the investor, but there are added costs to do this. Moving art from place to place can be expensive. Shipping insurance can be 2% of the value of the piece. So moving a million dollar painting to your summer home or anywhere such as an auction house could cost $20,000. Although fine art insurance in the home is not quite as expensive, a major collection represents a large annual insurance expense.

Liquidity issues

The secondary market for investment grade art has greatly evolved over the past fifty years, and with internet technology in the last ten years, the process of selling art has become more efficient. Nevertheless, to realize full value for a piece of art requires placing the art in the right auction at the right time. So if the investor requires immediate cash, she or he may have to sell the work at a significant discount. High transaction costs and discounts can significantly reduce the gain from any sale.

Expertise

Since the art market is primarily unregulated, knowledge and expertise in art is crucial. Depending on a dealer or anyone else who is selling art is asking for trouble. Most people do not have the time that is required to develop this expertise, and hiring a consultant just adds another cost to the investment.

Diversification

Although diversification of asset portfolio is probably the most significant financial reason for investing in art, there are some disadvantages of art investing compared to other alternatives. In time of financial uncertainty, investors turn to gold and other precious metals as safe haven investments in large part because of fears with money based assets. Besides the fear of declining asset values, there is the fear of illiquid assets, and liquidity is a major problem with art.

The acquisition of investment grade art always requires substantial investment. To achieve diversification goals, the investor must not only diversify asset types, but also diversify in the type. Acquiring a single million dollar painting will increase risk rather than reducing it. Thus, the investor must acquire additional pieces of art to reduce the risk in this asset class. Even for the wealthiest of investors, diversifying with art involves substantial investment.

Summary

Why not invest in art?

There are plenty of reasons as I have indicated above. I would suggest that purely on financial considerations, investing in art is not the wisest of courses for most individuals. However, when you add the pleasure of art collecting into the equation, art investment may be worthwhile when you combine both the financial and the aesthetic appreciation. Finally, many are intrigued with the more speculative components of art acquisition, such as the pleasure of finding and purchasing an early Pollock or Basquiat.

Evaluating art

As an art appraiser for over twenty years, I break down art into several major categories for evaluation.

Decorative art

As the name implies decorative art was created for decorative purposes. Most of it is reproductive, either lithographic or giclée. However, some of the art is original, and on occasion, the art has been commissioned by an interior decorator or designer. The reproductive pieces are usually moderate in cost whereas the commissioned original pieces can be quite expensive to purchase, but has little resale value. These pieces may bear a signature, but often the name is fictitious.

Because these pieces have been created and purchased for a decorative purpose, the resale value of the art is much less than the purchase price. Obviously, this art has little investment value.

Collectible art

I place most art in the category of collectible art. By collectible, I do not infer anything about its value, but simply that someone may find it worthy of being collected. Thus, even art created by a dabbler to hang in his or her own home is collectible.

I further breakdown collectible art into subcategories that are more meaningful. These subcategories include anonymous art, unknown art, established art and distinguished art.

Anonymous art

Again as the name implies anonymous art is art that we do not know the identity of the artist. In most of my appraisals there are pieces that are anonymous. Because they are anonymous, it does not mean that the pieces are not well painted. It just means that we do not know for certain who the artist was.

In art, the signature means everything, a great painting from anonymous artist appraises for less than an inferior painting from an identified established artist.

Some of the greatest artists of history painted pictures that for one reason or not, were never signed. And even if we recognize the work as probably belonging to a specific artist, the prospect of authenticating the piece to a specific artist is always difficult and expensive. So in most cases the artwork can termed "attributed to" or "school of" a particular artist. For instance, a painting may be described as "attributed to Rembrandt." Sometimes even paintings which are signed are given the "attributed to" designation, because there is not absolute proof that the artist painted the piece.

I recently appraised a painting that bore the signature of Albert Bierstadt. The signature on the painting matched Bierstadt's and the style was recognizable as Bierstadt's, but the owner had no evidence of its authenticity. This evidence is called its "provenance," which is documentation of the creation and ownership history of the work of art. The owner of the painting was attempting to sell the work at auction, but is value was severely compromised by this lack of authenticity.

The auction house that sold the piece identified it as "attributed" to Bierstadt, and the sale price was about a third of what an authenticated Bierstadt would have sold for. The owner of the piece could have attempted to have the piece authenticated and included in the artist's catalogue raisonné, which is an authoritative listing of an artist's paintings. This list is often developed by the estate of the artist or a board of experts with an interest in the artist's work. Unfortunately, there is not a recognized catalogue raisonné for every artist, and even when one exists, the process of have a painting included without provenance is difficult and lengthy.

When a painting is reminiscent of a particular artist and there is very little evidence that the artist painted the piece, it can be designated as a painting "of the school of Rembrandt." This designation is used even when the artist was never known to "school" anyone. Art of this designation carries much less value than the "attributed to" designation.

In most cases, anonymous art was painted by artists who did not feel compelled to sign their work. Artists who created work to be sold rarely left them unsigned and when they did it was matter of oversight rather than intention.

There is a presumption by many people that if a piece is old, especially very old pieces that its age implies high value. All we can say about an old painting is that it's old, and bad paintings were painted two-hundred years ago as they are today.

What gives value to art is the signature of the artist. If there is no signature, the value is severely diminished.

Unknown art

Unknown art is art that we can identify the artist, but the artist has no reputation or history . As an art appraiser, the majority of the pieces that I come upon in evaluating a collection are from unknown artists. It is a misconception that most artists create a reputation. In reality, probably less than one percent of one percent of those who paint or have painted ever create a reputation. There are probably 10 million Americans who are painting today. Most of them are signing their paintings. So the question is: "How many of these ten million artists will be recognized in a hundred years?"

The answer: "Not many."

Established art

Established art is art created by artists who have established some reputation, and there is a market for their work. If they are living, the artists are probably represented by galleries, and the more prestigious their galleries, the greater their art value.

These artists may not have established much of a secondary market history with few auction sales. The artwork may sell for high prices in the galleries, but these pieces are often difficult to resell and whose auction prices are much below their gallery prices. As investments, these pieces are not very liquid and very difficult to sell in the short term.

The reality is that few living artists will ever achieve the status of investment grade. If the collector is older than the artist, there is little chance of real asset appreciation for this art in the collector's life.

When an artist dies there is an assumption the value of their work rises immediately and dramatically. This may be the case for highly respected artists who have already demonstrated significant auction sales. But artists with lesser reputations may sink into obscurity with little value or market for their work.

Somewhere between established art and investment grade art is what I call *distinguished* art. This is art from living artists whose work sells for high prices, and those prices have begun to be seen in secondary market auctions. These are usually artists well into their latter years, and their prolificacy has slackened. Although these artists represent some uncertainty regarding future valuations of their work, their art may have real speculative value. Often when a distinguished artist dies, there is a spike in the value of their work.

Emerging and speculative art

Emerging art as the name implies, is the art of artists who are relatively new to the art scene. In most cases, these artists are young but also could be "late-bloomers." They are probably represented by a few galleries and have begun to receive some national recognition. Their price points may be relatively low but rising. For the new investor-collector without a huge art budget, this art has the most potential and would be classified as speculative.

It is the challenge for the collector to determine which of these artists represents the highest potential. There is no easy set of criteria that can accurately applied to determine future success for emerging artists. However there are some guidelines. The work should be devoid of traditional reference. What is valuable in the future will not be art from the past. The art should be identified with a contemporary art movement such as Street Art with the artist recognized as one of the movement's leading members, which in the case of Street Art would be Banksy. The successful collector must become extremely versed in whatever movement in which he invests, and it is helpful that they have developed a personal relationship with its major artists.

Investment grade art

Each year, thousands of pieces of art are sold at auctions in the United States, Europe and Asia. Of these pieces, a small percentage of the work is what I call investment grade art. Unlike bonds and stocks there are no official organizations, such as Standard and Poor's, that offer ratings for the art. The auctions, themselves, may indicate high and low price estimates for the piece, but price in itself does not indicate whether a piece of art is investment grade.

Investment grade art is art produced by artists who have established extensive auction history with consistently high prices. In most cases the major auction houses, such as Christie's and Sotheby's have sold their work. These artists are major artists with many of them considered historic. Rembrandt, Van Gogh, Monet, Cezanne and more recently Jackson Pollock and Willem de Kooning are such artists. Although no set of criteria will include every piece of investment grade art, the following criteria should provide a basis for evaluating pieces.

Extensive auction records

The artist should have extensive auction records with some sales at both the major auctions of Christie's and Sotheby's. If the art has not sold at these major auction houses, then the art probably has not reached investment grade. There are regional artists who have strong secondary market history may also qualify., but such artists are the exception.

High sale prices

The artist should have auction prices that exceed $100,000 and for truly top grade art, the prices should exceed $1 million. It was not too long ago when a $10 million painting was newsworthy. Today, a sale does evoke much conversation unless it tops $100 million.

In evaluating artists for investment, a positive sign is one who has achieved his high price recently. However, in examining auction records, aberrations can occur where a painting is sold for double the artist's previous highest price. This may just indicate an overly enthusiastic collector who just had to have the painting.

Price consistency

It is the nature of the art market that the prices vary considerably even for the same artist with similar paintings. There is no escaping such volatility. However, this variance should not be too extreme. A $100,000 painting from an artist who has sold paintings for a half-million dollars may seem like a steal, but if the artist has had recent sales of $50,000 for similar pieces it would give some reason to reconsider the purchase.

Positive price trend

Overall, investment grade art is characterized by rising prices. Several art auction results sites provide trend analysis for artists. Depending on the period and category of the art, prices for investment grade art has risen between 4-10% per year. Disclaimers to investors often state that previous performance is not guarantee for future performance. In the art market, it is a good indicator. There are artists who have experienced a downward trend in their prices, and for the cautious investor, these artists should be avoided.

Provenance and catalogue raisonné

There should be little question regarding the authenticity of a piece of investment grade art. The history of a piece of art from creation to current ownership is what we call its "provenance." Provenance serves as title insurance. If the history of a painting is well-documented, a buyer can feel relatively comfortable with its authenticity (although art sales history is rife with instances of art deceptions.).

A catalogue raisonné is another vehicle to establish authenticity. A catalogue raisonné is an authoritative listing and description of an artist's paintings. Often the estate of the artist will develop and maintain such a catalogue. Sometimes, it may be an academic organization or group of experts that maintain a catalogue. If a piece of art has little or no provenance, an owner may seek to have the piece authenticated and included in a catalogue raisonné.

The value of a piece of art that has no provenance and not included in a recognized catalogue raisonné is severely depreciated. Of course an art buyer may speculate on such a piece with the hope of getting it authenticated. New collectors often have the belief that an appraisal can serve as an authentication. When the authenticity of a piece of art is in question, only an expert authentication can validate the artwork, but even in these cases, the fact that the piece required authentication may have a depressing effect on its value. The surest bet is strong provenance.

Summary

In short, investment grade art is high priced and supported by extensive auction records including the major auction houses. The artist's prices should be rising., and the particular piece is well documented with a solid provenance.

Appraisals and authentications

The value of art is purely subjective. I have been asked many times why a particular artist or piece of art is valued as it is. My answer: "Art is what people will pay for it."

The value of art is subject to manipulation by its sellers. Although appraisals can be helpful, they can be misleading and sometimes even fraudulent. As an art appraiser, I have had collectors show me appraisals for artwork that significantly overvalue the art. Recently, a collector wanted me to reappraise a Norman Rockwell print, which he had a 1970 appraisal stating the print was worth $70,000. He was optimistic a new appraisal would push that value even higher. He was not too pleased to receive my appraisal of $750.

There are four major reasons that people seek an art appraisal. The most common reason is to investigate whether they have sufficient and proper insurance coverage for their collection. Secondly, estate and divorce settlements will usually require an appraisal. Thirdly, owners are considering a possible sale of their art, and wish to know its value. Fourthly, they are considering a charitable donation of their art for which the IRS may require an appraisal. Then, there are those who are simply curious about the value of a piece or pieces of art. The reason for the appraisal determines the type of appraisal and the choice of the appraiser.

For insurance purposes, a replacement value appraisal is usually provided. For most other purposes, a fair market value appraisal is usually the choice. An appraisal that doesn't indicate the type of appraisal is certainly questionable. Appraisals from galleries of artists whom they represent are often of this type, and reflect the price they wish to sell the art. They want to demonstrate that the work of a specific artist has shown a steady increase in price. When you try to resell the work back to the gallery, it will give you a real idea of its true value.

Types of appraisals

Fair Market Value: Fair market value (FMV) is the price that the art would sell for on the open market between a willing buyer and a willing seller, with neither being required to act and both have reasonable knowledge of the relevant facts. If there is a restriction on donated art, the FMV will reflect this restriction. This is the appraisal value that usually applied to charitable donations and estate values.

Replacement Value: Replacement value (RV) is the amount it would cost to replace an item with one of similar and like quality purchased in the most appropriate marketplace within a limited amount of time. This is the highest of the appraised values and is applied primarily to insurance coverage.

Market Value: Market value (MV) is the value realized, net of expenses by a willing seller disposing of the art in a competitive and open market to a willing buyer with both being reasonably knowledgeable of all relevant facts, and neither being under any constraint to buy or sell.

Liquidation Value: Liquidation value (LV) is the value realized in a sale situation under forced or limiting conditions and some time constraints. Appraisals for bankruptcy are usually the liquidation type.

Selecting an appraiser

Selecting a appraiser depends on many factors. Since the work should be visually inspected by the appraiser, it is best to find an appraiser near you. Since you are seeking the most accurate appraisal possible, it is important to find the most qualified appraiser for your kind of art. Since the cost of an appraisal depends on the time required, it is always wise to find an appraiser who specializes in the particular art. An expert in antique Chinese brush painting may be able to perform an appraisal in an hour that may take a general appraiser many hours.

Choosing an appraiser for charitable donation purposes deserves special attention since the Internal Revenue guidelines outline appraiser requirements, especially if the value of the donation is over $5000. The IRS requires what they call a "qualified" appraisal, and the appraiser must be certified. Although many requirements and restrictions are outlined, the most significant is that the appraiser must be certified by a recognized appraisal organization. The IRS also requires the appraiser to certify the authenticity of the work. Thus, if an appraisal value is expected to exceed $5000, not only must the appraiser be certified but he or she must also be qualified to certify the authenticity of the piece.

Appraisal fees

The cost of an appraisal ranges from as low as $25 to over $300 an hour. So selecting the right appraiser is not only a matter of the accuracy of the appraisal, but also the cost of the appraisal. It makes no sense to spend $600 appraising a $500 painting. In many cases, gallery appraisers will offer price evaluations at a rate less than a formal appraisal. Price evaluations are useful and cost efficient when the collector intends to sell the work and simply wishes to get some idea of how to price it for sale.

Before an appraisal is initiated the appraiser should provide you with his or her hourly rate, plus some estimate of the time required. If the appraiser cannot furnish you with such an estimate, it suggests the appraiser does not have experience in this particular area of art. Some appraisers require a deposit with signed approval to pursue the appraisal; for others, the process may be more informal.

Appraising your own art

Although you cannot appraise your own art for insurance or donation purposes, you can research the value of your art easily on the web. The first step is identifying the artist. No matter how exquisitely the artwork is produced, it has little value if the artist cannot be identified. Most pieces are signed by the artist, usually on the bottom right or left, but sometimes the signature is on the back of the painting. Unfortunately, many artist's signatures are difficult to decipher. So you may have to include several variations of the spelling to locate the right artist. To complicate the problem is that some artists sign their paintings with initials. There are a few sites that reference artist initials with names, but the probability of success is not high.

If you know the name of the artist, a web search should find references to the artist. If the initial research uncovers nothing, then it is a good probability the artist has little reputation and hence little value. It is surprising how often the search will uncover information on the artist, even some fairly obscure ones. The search may link to galleries and brokers who sell the particular artist's work. In some cases, the sites may have prices displayed, or you may have to email the gallery or broker requesting price information. Galleries are much more responsive to collectors who are seeking to purchase a piece than to collectors who are simply seeking information. It may be best to identify yourself as a buyer, not a seller. You can always re-contact the gallery to offer the piece for sale or consignment.

In the case of deceased artists, most collectible artists will be found in such searches and there should be links to auction sales information sites which provide sales results. These sites also provide the name of the auction, the date of the auction and the final sales price. Many also show images of the painting and may include a sample of the artist's signature. These sites charge for this information, but most offer a one-day pass for under $20.

Auction prices are lower than gallery retail prices, and are a better indicator of the price that you may ultimately receive for the painting. If selling the art is the primary motivation for the appraisal, this auction investigation will not only provide some information into sales value, but also those auction houses that deal in a specific artist. Different auctions will fetch different prices for art. Part of the research is to locate the auctions that have a greater success in selling the artist — success being determined by the prices the auction gets for the artist's work.

Authentications and appraisals

Appraising and authenticating are often confused. A piece of art is authenticated to determine the authenticity of a piece of art. That is, the art is what it is claimed to be. Authentication requires the services of an art expert or experts in the field of the particular artist. The process of authenticating a piece of art is complex and time-consuming, and therefore expensive. Artwork that may have significant value can make the investment in an authentication worthwhile. The authentication process begins with a physical examination and testing of the component materials of art. The piece is subjected to several tests including: infrared tests, wood lamp tests, a study of the pigments, etc. The purpose of these physical tests is to insure the work was completed at the time of the assumed artist.

These physical tests are followed by the work of graphologists who examine the signature and any other writing on the work that might be attributed to the artist.

Then, experts examine the work in context to other work of the artist as well as work from other similar artists who painted within the same time frame. There will also be an examination of any documents associated with the painting which is called its "provenance." The authenticators will also research on the artist's life to discover any mention of such a painting. This would include exhibition catalogs, gallery records, etc.

After this thorough examination, the expert or panel of experts will determine whether an authentication is possible. In many cases, the art cannot be authenticated. The cost of authentication can run into the thousands of dollars so the process should not be undertaken unless there is solid foundation to believe the work has been created by a significant artist.

Investigate before you act

If the collector is considering the sale of the work, this research will provide a valuable reference of galleries and auction houses. Even if the collector is seeking an appraisal for insurance or donation purposes, the research provides the collector on information which pieces in the collection that should be appraised and which are not worth the appraisal cost.

Broker and gallery margins have severely declined because of the easy availability of sales information on the internet. When collectors seek to sell or buy a piece of art, they generally have some knowledge of the potential value of the art. Collectors who do not do this research will be at a great disadvantage when negotiating with dealers.

Buying art

It has never been easier to buy art. The internet with its internationalization has greatly expanded the sources of art for collectors. Although the supply of art has greatly expanded, the availability of investment grade art has shrunk with the increased competition for its acquisition by private and institutional buyers. Sources for investment grade art are still primarily the large auction houses and a few private dealers and galleries.

Although the supply and availability for investment grade art has changed little, the opposite is the case for speculative art. With the assistance from the internet, the art speculator can acquire art from virtually any artist on the globe. For the art buyer, greater choice is usually a positive opportunity, but with the thousands of potential artists to choose from, finding the right artist has become much more of a challenge.

Galleries

For the last two centuries, art galleries have been the dominant source of art, especially for contemporary and emerging art. With the development of the internet, galleries have begun to lose their dominance as other alternatives have appeared such as regional auction houses and online auctions,

The first commercial galleries appeared in the mid-Nineteenth Century. The gallery most often noted as the first gallery was that of Ernest Gambart. Belgian-born Gambart arrived in London is 1840. Originally a dealer in art prints, he became London's most prestigious publisher of prints of such artists as John Everett Millais, Dante Gabriel Rossetti and William Powell Frith. He would also bring European artists Lawrence Alma-Tadema and Rosa Bonheur to London where he represented their original art and was greatly responsible for the success of their art careers.

Galleries have changed little over the last 175 years. Artists consign their work to galleries who sell the work and receive commissions for the sales. The commission is negotiated and usually ranges between 50% for emerging artists to 25% for the top-ranked established artist.

Some galleries may only deal in the work of deceased artists. In this case, galleries secure much of their inventory from individual collectors who consign or sell their work. Commissions for consigned pieces are also negotiated but are basically the same range as the commissions for contemporary artists. These galleries may also be active buyers at auctions. Gallery commissions for consigned work are higher than commissions the collector would pay an auction house.

Of all of the sources of art that a collector can access, purchasing art from galleries is the most costly. With high overhead and operating costs, galleries require high commissions to operate. Purchasing a piece from a gallery might cost twice that of purchasing the work directly from the artist. And if the gallery secured the artwork at auction, they are going to add a hefty premium to their sales price.

Galleries offer other services and amenities to the collector that may justify the additional price of the art. For the art investor, these additional acquisition costs are not justified. There are occasions where a gallery has exclusive control of an artist's inventory, which makes alternative purchases impossible, so for the investor there is little choice if they must have that artist's work. But these situations are rare, and for most collector-investors, these situations should be avoided.

Auction houses

The internet has led to an explosion of art auctions. Added to the brick and mortar auction houses are hundreds of other online auction and art sales sites. The development of internet auction technology has allowed even the smallest auction houses to expose their lots to an international market.

Before the internet, small regional auctions were a lucrative source of acquiring investment grade art. For instance, a dealer may discover that a painting from a Hudson River artist was being auctioned in Topeka. There may be little interest for the work in Topeka, and the piece could be purchased for a fraction of the price that it would fetch in New York. Then, the dealer could quickly flip the piece to a New York dealer or auction house. Today, the same auction house could offer the same piece, but instead of a few local buyers at the auction, there may be hundreds of dealers and collectors around the country who will be bidding online. Not only will the piece sell for a considerably higher price, but the hammer price will be recorded on the dozens of online auction result sites. So if the piece comes up for bidding at a subsequent auction, the potential buyers will see the previous sales price. So for art sellers, the internet has been a boom, but for dealers, it has resulted in diminished profit margins.

With declining availability of investment grade art, and especially art of historic masters, there are few bargains to be found. The buyer premium for the major auction houses are as high as 25%. With art prices increasing around 4% year, it takes five years to make back the buyer premium. These financial realities certainly limit the prospects of significant profits.

Despite the declining auction opportunities for dealers, they still must resort to auction houses to maintain their sales inventories. Art collector-investors face dealer competition at even the smaller auction houses, but the auction prices will always be lower than the collector would have had to pay at a gallery. Thus, auction houses, especially small regional houses, remain a real possibility for the art collector-investor.

Online sales sites

There is no shortage of online internet art sales sites. Ebay, the most successful online auction, has virtually thousands of pieces of art available for bid every day. The great majority of the pieces have little collectible value. It is not uncommon to find work being offered of recognized artists such as Picasso, Dali and Chagall. Many of these are prints and a great majority of them are fakes. No one is going to sell an original Edward Hopper for $700. Novice collectors may be tempted to take a chance on such pieces, but the rewards are rare.

There are dozens of smaller online art auction sites, but the model is flawed. Potential buyers are usually reluctant to buy a piece of art unseen for more than a few hundred dollars. Recently both Sotheby's and Christie's have launched online auctions. The art is of a higher grade than you normally encounter from other sites, but their highest grade investment art is not going to be shifted away from their live auctions.

There are also hundreds of online gallery sites. Most of these offer art from unknown emerging artists. A few of these sites offer some interesting work from emerging artists, but the overall outlook does not appear positive.

Dealers

Dealers are not subject to the overhead expenses of either galleries or auctions so they should be able to sell art with lower profit margins. Dealers are not in the business to inventory paintings, and in many cases they won't acquire work unless they already have a buyer lined up to purchase the piece. Also, most dealers do not possess the kind of financial resources of the major art investors. They make their money by quickly turning over inventory. The reality is that the prices dealers charge depends greatly on the individual circumstance of the dealer. Often, a dealer may have to make a sale to facilitate another deal, and in those cases may dispose art for their cost or even lower.

Most collector-investors interface with a group of dealers who will periodically bring deals to them. If the dealer is desperate to make a sale, the buyer is in a strong position to negotiate a very attractive purchase. However, sometimes the deals that are too good to pass up are exactly the ones to avoid, especially with dealers with whom the investor is unacquainted.

Like the situation with galleries, there are dealers who exclusively represent a specific artist so acquiring work from this artist places the buyer at a disadvantage in the negotiations. Despite the potential jeopardies when working with dealers, they offer a source of art at prices below those of auctions and galleries.

Estate and garage sales, resale shops, etc.

Twenty years ago art dealers would scour backwoods antique stores looking for undiscovered art jewels. Today, some dealers continue these searches, but finding significant collectible work is becoming increasingly difficult. Owners and managers of resale shops nearly always consult the internet before pricing and displaying work. Occasionally, they might overlook a piece or are unable to read the artist's signature, but this is rare.

Estate sales were once fertile ground for finding collectible pieces, but many estate sales are managed by professional sales companies who are fairly diligent in investigating the art in such estates. There are pieces that do slip by when sales are managed by family who are just interested in clearing out the estate.

Individuals conducting yard and garage sales are not always so diligent in selling pieces of art. Every few months, one will read an article about a masterpiece that was purchased at a yard sale for a few dollars. Indeed, these things occur, but people also win the lottery. Serious collectors have better things to do with their time than spending their Saturdays driving from one garage sale to the next.

Other collector-investors

The number of major art collector-investors is really quite small, and like any small community, there is a fair amount of awareness of each other. Many of the major acquisitions are between such collectors, who want to avoid paying commissions on multi-million dollar paintings. Often these transactions are aided by dealers and auction houses, but they are paid transaction fees, not commissions.

By avoiding commissions and the assortment of other transaction fees, selling and buying directly from other collectors is very advantageous to both the buyer and seller. However, buying from another collector means that the buyer does not have some of the legal protections afforded by dealer purchases.

Buying from other collectors on popular online auction sites is quite another matter. Internet art selling is rife with dangers. There are many scammers who prey on unsuspected buyers, and even honest sellers may not actually be aware of the authenticity of the work they are peddling. One will often encounter art sales opportunities on the internet that appear too good to pass up, but these are just the ones to avoid.

Artists

Virtually, every artist sells work out of their studio. This includes the greats like Picasso, Matisse and Monet. For the collector-investor who is collecting contemporary art, the most cost-efficient source is directly from the artist. Although artists may be bound by their agreements with their galleries not to sell directly to collectors, many ignore these agreements. There is a feeling among many artists that galleries do not deserve the commissions they charge, and with declining gallery sales, these feelings have become accentuated.

There are artists so adverse to social interactions that they would never open their studio to collector visits, but this is a small minority. There is a huge ego element in the art community, and many artists cannot avoid an opportunity to have their egos stroked. Then, there are artists who simply enjoy the pleasure of human interaction, and enjoy collector visitors even without an expectation of sales.

Once a collector has established a personal and sales relationship with the artist, studio visits come with an expectation of a sale. Artists often come to value these relationships purely on a personal basis, and have shown their appreciation with gifts. For example,

Jean-Michael Basquiat was prone to scribble out a small drawing as a thank you to a friend. The current market for these simple drawings command tens of thousands.

After time, collectors can develop reputations within a certain community of art genre. The reputation will lead to studio invitations from new artists. Of course galleries resent the artist-collector relationships outside of the gallery, but if the artist is popular they will be reluctant to challenge them.

What collectors pay for work at the artist's studio depends upon many factors: the artist's success, the inventory, the artist's relationship with the gallery, and the artist's immediate financial situation. The collector's personal relationship with the artists also plays a significant part. Artists who have a great demand for their work have little motivation to discount their work while emerging artists, even the most promising, are usually in need of sales. Prolific artists may have a studio stuffed with paintings while slow-producing artists may only have a few pieces. The very prolific artist may welcome the opportunity to rid the studio of a few pieces, whereas the assiduous, slow-producing artist would be reluctant to part with any piece. Even in those cases where the collector is obliged to pay the gallery price, the purchase can be rationalized on the basis of securing some of the finest work of the artist before it's released to a gallery. However in most cases, the price that a piece is offered will be much less than what the collector would have to pay the gallery

The successful collector-artist relationship does not lend itself to haggling over prices. If the collector expresses interest in a particular piece, the collector is not advised to attempt a bargain. The collector wants to be welcomed in the studio — not a skinflint whose appearance the artist dreads.

Buying from emerging artist is always speculative. The collector may have to hold the works for decades before the art can be sold profitably. Most of these acquisitions will yield little except the pleasure of supporting an artist's life, but for many collectors this may be sufficient. Because of the future uncertainties of such purchases, the collector should select a genre of work he or she appreciates for the art will be around for at least a few years.

Conclusions...

For the collector investing in established artists with strong secondary art records, buying from dealers and auction houses will be a necessary option. Buying directly from the artist can be the most rewarding, both financially and personally.

Then there are those who relish the social opportunities that are provided by galleries. If you enjoy schmoozing with gallery directors and other collectors, then galleries may be your choice, but there is a price for such schmoozing.

Selling art

There is a maxim in the art business, "It is always easier to buy art than it is to sell it."

Certain kinds of art have virtually no sales potential beyond the realm of garage and yard sales. This includes artwork in which the identity of the artist cannot be determined such as case of paintings that are unsigned or have illegible signatures. Even paintings where the artist can be identified may have little value unless the artist has some reputation and that reputation is supported by verifiable auction sales. For every 1000 artists who create art, perhaps only one has real resale possibility.

Original artwork from contemporary artists who are currently being marketed by either the artist or gallery may have some value, but the resale value will be significantly less than the artist's current gallery prices. Galleries representing living artists will be reluctant to purchase or even take on consignment work of these artists, and when they do, the consignment comes with a hefty commission.

Reproductive art such as lithographs, etchings, giclées are always difficult to sell and usually do not command much value. This is particularly the case of reproductive art from contemporary artists. In most cases, the seller would be fortunate to receive 20% of the current retail rate. There are only a few artists whose prints command great value. These include such historically important reproductive artists such as Rembrandt, Chagall, and Toulouse-Lautrec. Reproductive art is also the most susceptible to counterfeiting. Dali and Picasso and Chagall are frequent examples.

Deceased second-tier artists' work may have value if there is auction history supporting sales. In most cases, these pieces are sold through regional and secondary auction houses — not the major national auction houses.

Selling Art

Selling investment grade art utilizes the same outlets as the purchasing of art with the exception that artists are rarely interested in repurchasing their work. Art auctions are the most common venue for art sales, but some collectors also sell their work through galleries and brokers. For multi-million dollar artwork, collectors often sell work to other collectors to avoid high commissions and other selling fees.

Auctions

The great majority of investment grade art is sold through the major and secondary art auctions with Christie's and Sotheby's the major auction houses. Depending on the expected sales price, the seller's commission will range between 5-15% while for major million dollar pieces; the selling commission may be even lower. However, the buyer commission, called the buyer's premium, will be much higher — sometimes as much as 25%. The buyer's premium affects the seller as well. Adding 25% to the hammer price of the art has a constraining effect on the purchase of the art. Many multi-million dollar art sales are private because neither the seller nor the buyer want to include that 25% commission in the acquisition price.

Besides the sales commissions, there are a myriad of other expenses the seller bears when selling through auctions. These include insurance, catalog, and photography fees. The most onerous of fees is the buy-in which is charged to the seller if the item does not sell. The buy-in fee is usually around 5%. This also points to other major problem with auctions — the uncertainty of sales. With many auctions, there may be a six month window from initial contact to the actual sale. So not only is the art tied up for six months, but the seller is faced with another lengthy delay and additional fees if the piece has to be returned to auction.

Auctions also have rescission clauses in their consignment agreements that allow the auction to cancel a sale if there are disputes over authenticity or other problems. Most rescission clauses have time limits for their exercise, but some may be for a year or more. Because of this, the seller may be liable for return of the sales proceeds months after the sale.

Despite all of these potential problems and fees, auction houses remain the best alternative for selling the majority of investment grade work. However, the choice of auction is of paramount importance, which is covered in the next chapter.

Dealers

The savvy art collector-investor is usually aware of the dealers who specialize in the genre of art in the collector's portfolio. Often these dealers may have clients who are seeking work from artists who the collector-investor has available for sale. In some cases, these clients may even be willing to purchase the desirable pieces at a premium. Whatever the situation, contacting dealers regarding potential works for sale is always a wise decision. Even if the dealer does not have immediate buyers, circulating information about available work for sale can generate interest in the art.

Dealer commissions may be less than those charged by auction houses and the seller avoids other auction expenses. More importantly, sales are often immediate, avoiding the uncertainty of auction sales. For these reasons, selling work through a dealer may be the optimum choice.

Consigning work to dealers can be problematic, especially with dealers whom the collector is unfamiliar. A dealer is going to require an exclusive consignment agreement, and most will require a minimum term of six months. Also, the dealer will have physical possession of the work so the collector has lost a great deal of control over his asset. Finally, even if the piece sells, there can be problems getting paid immediately. There are also legal issues involving dealers which are discussed later. The most salient point is once the dealer sells consigned work, the owner of the art has little recourse against the new buyer if the dealer fails to pay the consignor.

Over time, collector-investors develop a network of dealers with whom they do business. These relationships require trust for both the collector and the dealer. Trusts can always be betrayed, but the collector is inviting trouble when working with dealers they don't know, and even worse, dealers they do not trust.

Galleries

Galleries dealing in investment grade art are always seeking to add to their inventory. Because of their high overhead, galleries require higher margins on their sales than do dealers. Collectors selling or consigning work to galleries should expect to pay higher commissions than from dealers or auctions. Collectors solicit galleries because of their high visibility. When researching potential buyers for a particular artist's work, the collector will much more likely to find galleries than individual dealers.

Because of the emergence of the internet and plethora of auction result sites, collectors are much more aware of the value of their work. This awareness has had the effect of reducing sales margins for dealers and galleries. A typical gallery may take a 40% commission on consignments, and if they purchase the work, they may want a discount of 60%. These are steep commissions and discounts, but for the collector who needs an immediate sale, it may be the only alternative.

Most galleries prefer to accept paintings on consignment. This option is the least favorable for the collector. The consignment agreement is going to tie up the painting for a longer period of time, and like an auction there is no guarantee the gallery will sell the piece. When an auction sells a piece, the likelihood of the consignor not getting paid is remote. The same cannot be said for galleries. There are few businesses with a higher failure rate than galleries, and often when cash is tight, consignors are the last to get paid.

Of all of the sales options for the collector-investor, galleries are the least attractive. If the work is consigned, the commission rate will be high, and if the work is purchased, the value will be severely discounted.

Artists

Artists, especially those who are selling their own art, will occasionally repurchase or take consignments of their own art. This is a rare situation, but every artist has a few pieces that he or she regrets selling, and would be open to reacquiring. Occasionally, enterprising artists will offer to take a piece on consignment. All of the disadvantages of consigning to a gallery apply to consigning with an artist.

Other collectors

Many multi-million dollar sales of art are between collectors. There are no commissions to be paid which means considerable savings for both parties. In the majority of these instances, the sale was instigated by the buyer, who may have admired the work in the collector's home. In most of these cases, the seller and the buyer are friendly, if not friends, so there is usually little haggling over the price. Many collectors wish to keep their collection out of the public eye, and such sales do not come under public scrutiny.

Doing business with friends always involves threats to the friendship and art is no exception. Questions of authenticity and value which arise later can certainly jeopardize friendships. From a purely financial perspective, selling and buying art from other collectors is a very cost-efficient way to sell and acquire art.

Auctions

Once you have evaluated the art and have determined that it has auction value, the next step is to choose the auction to consign the piece. The choice of auction will have a significant influence on the selling price of the art. Choosing the wrong auction at the wrong time can result in no sale or a sale at a disappointing price.

Generally speaking, the more prestigious the auction house, the higher the price you can expect to receive for your work. However, in order for Christie's or Sotheby's to have interest in handling the work, the piece must be a nationally recognized artist with some auction history — especially history with that auction house. If the piece is not of this quality, then you will have to select a secondary auction house to handle its sale.

If the artist has little or no auction history, then selling your work at any art auction becomes very problematic. In your initial research on the art, you should search for auctions that have sold the artist in the past. If an auction has sales history with a specific artist, then it is very probable that they would be interested in handling the work, and they may also have collectors who are interested in buying the work. If the pieces they have sold previously are similar to yours, then it gives you a fairly good estimate what your piece might sell for. Every auction and every piece of art is different, but this is one of the best indicators of sales potential.

For artists who have regional reputations and regional collectors, an auction that specializes in pieces from this region may yield superior performance than even the national auctions. For example, Louisiana artist George Louis Viavant painted wonderful pictures of Louisiana swamp birds and animals. Because of his association with Louisiana, a seller will probably have more success selling the work in New Orleans than in New York. Again, this conclusion should be verified with initial research.

With the development of national and international online auction bidding services such as LiveAuctioneers and ArtFact, even small regional auctions can attract buyers from all over the world. So when considering regional auction houses, it make sense to choose one that is affiliated with one or more of these services. Obviously, the larger the group of bidders, the greater the probability a piece will fetch a high price. Also, having a large contingent of bidders outside of the auction house discourages possible collusion among the live bidders.

The most obvious consideration in choosing an auction house is the commission they charge the seller, and to a certain degree the commission they charge the buyers. In most cases, the seller's commission will be between 10-25% depending on the sales price of the piece — the lower the price, the higher the commission rate. For very desirable pieces, selling above six figures, the selling commission may be negotiated even lower, since the major auction houses charge substantial buyer's premiums. Obviously, the seller is more concerned with the seller's commission than the buyer's commission, but if sellers know that 25% is going to be tacked on to the final price, it has a constraining influence on bidding behavior.

Besides the selling commission, the seller can also expect other charges from the auction. The seller can be charged for insurance, storage, photography, advertising, and some auctions charge even a fee if the piece does not sell. This last fee, called a buy-in fee, discourages sellers from putting high reserves on their work. It is not a happy seller who walks away from an auction without a sale, and with a significant fee to boot.

Before a collector consigns work, all of these additional charges should be shown on the consignment agreement, and discussed before signing the agreement. Unfortunately, this is not always the case leaving the consignor with some unpleasant surprises. Again, if the work is desirable, some of these charges can be negotiated and at times omitted.

All auction consignment agreements include verbiage that protects the auction house against any legal actions initiated by both the buyers and the sellers. For art sellers, the right of rescission is often overlooked and in some ways the most important. The right of rescission allows the auction to rescind any sale into the future. When an auction exercises that right, the buyer is returned his money and the seller is returned his art. Rescission rights offer some protection to buyers and also provide the auction protection against any legal action initiated against them by either the seller or the buyer. Some rescission provisions include time limits as short as a few days while others may extend for five years or indefinitely. Rescission provisions place the sale under a cloud of uncertainty. These provisions are included in most consignment agreements, but they may also be negotiated.

The timing of the auction can also affect price. Auctions in the fall yield better prices than auctions in the spring and summer. Specialized auctions that feature the kind of work you are offering will also yield better prices. For instance, a piece by Albert Bierstadt will sell better in an auction of Hudson River School painters than a general auction.

Shipping is another issue that the seller needs to consider. Crating and shipping a piece 2000 miles will be more costly than shipping a few hundred miles. And if the work does not sell, the seller must bear the return shipping and crating charges.

Once you have selected an auction, the next major decision is setting the reserve price. The reserve price is the lowest amount the seller will accept for the art. The auction house will set the expected range of prices for the work. For instance, that range may be between $20,000 – $30,000. So the reserve price will be some amount equal to or less than $20,000. Each seller's situation is different. In an estate settlement situation, the seller will be motivated to sell, and therefore set a very low or even no reserve for the work. Conversely, a professional dealer who sells regularly may not wish to dispose a piece without receiving a strong bid for the work. In this case, the reserve is going to be much closer to the minimum estimated price. Since the auction house wants to sell every piece in an auction, they will always recommend low reserves.

For individuals who may never sell another piece at auction, the experience can be very exciting, especially with high estimates for the piece. That excitement can be increased by the choice and location of an auction. An auction in Topeka is not the same as an auction in New York. Although your primary objective is to net as much from the sale as possible, maximizing the experience may also factor in your choice of auction.

The most significant development in art collecting in the past ten years has been the emergence of online auction bidding. Collectors can actively bid at hundreds of national and international auctions. Although there may be only a hundred bidders in the auction room, there may be thousands at their computer terminals.

Although the major international art auctions such as Christie's and Sotheby's maintain traditional live and telephone bidding, most of the secondary auction houses provide online bidding. Some of the online auctions have developed their own dedicated bidding technology, but most have subscribed to services offered by online bidding technology firms such as Live Auctioneers and ArtFact.

Not only do these firms provide technology, but they also provide client auction houses with promotional services to attract more bidders to the client auction sites.

A distinction must be made between auctions offering online bidding and those that are exclusively online. There are very few successful pure online auctions for art. eBay is the most recognizable and popular auction, but the preponderance of the art is from working artists selling inexpensive pieces. Others selling art on eBay include minor dealers here and internationally. There are few investment grade pieces offered on eBay, but they come with much uncertainty since there is no third party evaluating the pieces.

ArtNet has developed an online auction offering higher grade artwork, but the auction has generated mixed results. There are a handful of other online auctions, but again the investment quality of the art is lacking.

Bidding online with established auctions is a fairly simple process. The prospective bidder registers with the online bidding service, which transmits the information to the art auction. The art auction approves or disapproves the prospective buyer, and an email is sent to buyer indicating his or her status. In most cases, there is little financial information required of the prospective bidder, and most are approved. Of course, there is a possibility reneging by bidders, but this is a fairly rare occurrence. The prospective bidder logs on and bids with simple console settings. Most of these applications provide the bidder with information for distinguishing online bidders from live bidders. If the online bidder wins the auction, he or she is contacted by the auction house for payment. The buyer is charged the normal buyer's commission, and there may be an additional charge for the internet service. This is usually around 2-3%. There are shipping charges that will be added to the buyer's fees.

Another bidder service provided by these online firms is to notify potential bidders of upcoming auctions of artists and art which they may have interest. So a California collector who collects the Hudson River School painters has easy access to New England auction houses which specialize in this genre. Conversely, a New England collector has a chance to bid on work that might be available in California.

Another consequence of these online auctions is the increased availability of information regarding auction prices since most of these auctions report the results of their auctions to the subscription auction sites. Online auction service has benefited both sellers and buyers, but dealers have seen their profits erode as buyers and sellers have much more access to information for evaluating art.

Insurance

In any investment, a major objective is to minimize risk. Insurance is the most frequent instrument to protect investments. Art insurance provides coverage for very reasonable rates and should be secured regardless of the size of the art collection.

Many homeowners make the assumption that their art collection is covered under their homeowner's policy. Homeowner policies generally will not cover broken or lost items, provide out-of-home coverage, and have limitations on transportation. Collectors may also be shocked to learn that certain homeowner policies specifically exclude fine art items. In many cases, there is a limit on the coverage of individual pieces of art. Such limits can be under $1000. With this reality in mind, every individual who owns even a small collection of fine art should review his or her policy.

There are two kinds of art insurance: casualty and title. For most collectors, casualty insurance will probably be sufficient.

Casualty insurance

There are basically two types of art casualty insurance coverages: scheduled and blanket. With scheduled policies, each item is individually listed on the policy for a stated insured amount. Insurers usually require an appraisal or a recent invoice for an item's value. Blanket policies are policies that allow a collector to obtain coverage of items without specifically itemizing the objects. Most blanket policies will include a maximum limit per item. Casualty insurance covers theft, fire and water damage. Coverage for items in transit differ considerably among policies. Policies do not cover natural deterioration, such as fading or cracking caused by natural or artificial light.

The cost of fine art insurance is fairly in line with homeowner's insurance. However, premium costs can vary significantly, and one usually finds the best insurance values with companies that specialize in fine art insurance. Art insurance is one of the least expensive forms of insurance. Depending on the coverage, the cost can range between 2% to 4% of the value of the total collection. Thus, for a million dollar collection, the annual premium would be $2000 to $4000. The coverage can be individualized for each piece or it can cover the full collection. In most cases, the coverage is for the replacement value of the work, which is established initially by appraisal. Some policies may also provide coverage for potential increases in the value of the collection. Again, the extent of coverage will determine the premium cost.

Like all insurance policies, the cost depends on the value of the potential loss. The insurance company will require a current appraisal, and in certain cases recommend an appraiser to the client. The comprehensiveness of the appraisal depends on the value of the work. Appraisals for million dollar paintings come under much greater scrutiny by insurance underwriters while the appraisals for lesser valued artworks are usually accepted without reservation.

For insurance purposes, the type of appraisal needed is a replacement value appraisal. This appraisal values the art for the highest amount, and although this also will increase the insurance premiums, it insures full coverage. Whether your appraiser offers the service or you do it yourself, it is always beneficial to have a picture of your fine art items. This is particularly useful if the item is stolen.

When there is a claim, the appraised replacement value is usually accepted, but occasionally the insurance company may challenge the appraised value even though it was originally accepted. So pressuring appraisers to inflate values may actually backfire for the collector who has paid the premium based on the appraised value, but may not receive that value if it is discovered the appraised values were inflated.

The activities of the art collector will frequently involve the shipment of art to and from the home. Most home insurance does not fully cover shipment risks. Separate shipment insurance for fine art can be 2% or more of the value of the piece. So shipping a $100,000 painting to the auction house would cost the collector $2000, which may be more than the annual insurance premium for the entire art collection.

In terms of shipment coverage and policies, every insurer is different. For the active art investor, this issue deserves the most attention. The insurance company may restrict their coverage to include specified shippers or may require excessive shipping preparation.

Title insurance

The second kind of art insurance is art title insurance. When a person buys a home, the mortgage lender requires the buyer to purchase title insurance. Title insurance insures that the persons or persons who are selling the house have clear title to the property. Art title insurance works in the same way. It insures that the person or business who is selling the artwork has clear title to the art.

Most art transactions involve third parties who are arranging the sale. The third party may be a gallery, a broker or an auction house. In terms of the ownership of the art, there are two potential problems. First, the third party seller may not pay the owner of the art. In many cases the buyer will be legally forced to return the art to the owner with the only recourse for the buyer is to be compensated by the third-party seller. This scenario occurs all too frequently with gallery sales. The gallery owner may be corrupt or just financially desperate. In either case, the owner who consigned the painting never receives payment and then is forced to take legal action against both the gallery and the buyer.

The second problem is that the third party seller may sell work that is not actually owned by the consignor. In this case the rightful owner of the art can bring suit against everyone involved in the transaction including the buyer.

Art title insurance protects the buyer against such scenarios, but also protects the third party seller as well against a faulty consignor. The premium for art title insurance is about 2% of the sales price of the art and it is a one-time payment. Art title insurance is usually reserved for artwork that has significant value. It should be noted that title insurance does not cover problems in authenticity. Even if the seller knows the art is not authentic, title insurance does not protect the buyer. It only guarantees that the seller owns the piece, albeit a fraudulent piece.

Art insurance is a necessary expense for every art investor. For the active investor, shipping provisions in the casualty insurance are of foremost importance. In the case of major art acquisitions, title insurance is recommended regardless of the collector's confidence in the integrity of the seller.

Art and estate planning

For the art investor, art is an asset with the same considerations as the rest of the investor's financial portfolio including estate management. There are some unique provisions in the income tax code that apply specifically to art which the investor should be aware.

The motivations of the art investor are not coincidental with those of the art collector who may be interested in maintaining the collection after death. For the art collector, donating the collection to a museum or even starting his or her own museum are courses of action that do not usually apply to the investor whose motivations are primarily financial.

For the art investor, the primary decision deals with the disposal of the art collection, and the timing of that disposal. There are many factors that have to be included when considering the disposal of an art collection, and most of these have to deal with tax considerations. The primary decision is whether the collection should be disposed before or after death. There are many factors that go into determining the preferred course: the size and composition of the individual's estate, the long-term capital gains liability of the collection, the investor's own philanthropic desires and the attitude of the heirs toward the art.

The attitude of the heirs can often cause family problems if the desires of the heirs are not communicated. Many people are reluctant to discuss "after-death" matters, but when it comes to art collections they should be addressed.

The basis for art

At death the basis in the art is its fair market value, whereas before death, the basis is the investor's purchase price of the art. So if a person gives a gift before death, the basis of the art for the receiver is the same as the giver, and if the receiver should sell the art, he or she would be subject to the long-term collectibles tax. If an individual inherits a piece of art, the basis is its current fair market value, and there is no long-term collectible tax liability.

The size and composition of the estate

Current federal tax laws (2018) exempts $11.2 million from the taxable estate. Thus, for the collector with an estate valued under that figure, the estate will pay no taxes on the estate assets including the art. An estate valued over the exempted value will be taxed up to 40% of the amount.

If the estate is valued under the exempt value, disposal of the art is best postponed to after death – thus avoiding paying long-term capital gains

Capital gains liability on the art collection

The long-term capital gains has a federal tax rate of 28% for collectibles such as art. If the investor has realized significant growth in value of the collection, selling the collection before death will result in a high tax bill. If the collection has not realized significant gains in value, then there is little disincentive to dispose of the art before death.

The art attitude of the heirs and gift tax

The attitude of the heirs regarding the art also influences the decision. Certain heirs may wish to inherit all or selected pieces in the art collection. If the heirs express an interest in the art, the investor can include pieces of art in the inheritance provisions or even give gifts of the art while living. Annual gifts of under $14,000 are not subject to federal gift taxes.

The collector's philanthropic desires

The collector may desire to include certain charities and foundations in the estate disposition. Donating art to qualified charitable benefactors can reduce income and estate taxes. The amounts of these deductions depend on the status of the benefactor and in the income of the collector. Donations to museums provide the greatest deductions.

Although every art investor has a unique set of circumstances that apply to his or her estate considerations, certain generalizations can be stated given the current tax code. If the estate is under $11.2 million, it is better to dispose the collection after death since all of the assets are exempted from federal estate taxation. This is especially advisable when the art collection is subject to high long-term collectible gains tax. This would be the case regardless to the heirs' attitude toward the art.

UPDATE: The new federal tax code enacted in 2017 greatly reduces estate taxes. Thus, much of the decision regarding pre-death and post-death decisions have been obviated for capital gains taxes can be avoided by disposing the collection after death. The issue of capital gains tax is unclear. State estate taxes still exist, but for most tax considerations, these are not significant.

Tax codes are fairly stable but they are subject to change, there is no certainty whether that stability will remain given the recent politicalization of the tax code. New congressional makeups could reverse recent decisions.

Art and law

In the art business, legal issues pertain primarily to the transactions between dealer and collector. A dealer can be defined as any individual or company that is engaged in the commercial activity of buying and selling art. Besides private dealers, this would include galleries, auction houses and brokers. Most of the law surrounding these issues are codified in a set of statutes called the Uniform Commercial Code (UCC) which covers commercial transactions. It should be noted that the sale between two noncommercial individuals are not covered by the UCC.

Warranties of authenticity and title

When a collector purchases a piece of art, there are two major concerns. First, is the piece authentic and secondly does the seller have good title?

Authenticity means the item is what the dealer claims it to be. The description of the piece should be fully elaborated on the bill of sale. It should include the name of the artist, the title of the work, the medium and the physical size. For instance: Thomas Moran, "New Mexico Sunrise," 16 x 20," oil on canvas. The description may also include the condition of the art and a description of the frame. In the dealer's promotional material, it may state that the painting is "one of Moran's finest painting and his only New Mexico painting." Thus, to be authentic, the painting must have been actually painted by Thomas Moran with the physical dimensions as described. It should also be Moran's only New Mexico painting, but the opinionative statement that the painting is "one of Moran's finest," is called "puffing" and probably would not disqualify the painting even if other experts questioned that assessment.

The bill of sale constitutes the dealer's warranty for the painting.

If the painting was not painted by Moran or if he painted other New Mexico scenes, then the dealer has committed a breach of warranty which entitles the buyer to some compensation from the seller and legal recourse if the dealer refuses compensation. Because the bill of sale represents the core warranty for the item, it should be comprehensive in its description.

Although states differ in their laws, breach of warranty claims usually have to be filed within four years of the transaction. If the buyer learns, five years later the painting was determined not to be an original Moran, the purchaser would have no recourse unless he could prove the seller knew the piece was a fake. In that case, the seller could be subject to fraud charges.

A bill of sale is what is called an "expressed warranty." There are also "implied warranties," and the most important is the warranty of title. Rarely will a bill of sale have any verbiage regarding title, but when an item is sold by a dealer there is the legal implication that the dealer has good title for the work. The consignment agreement between the collector and dealer will stipulate that the collector indeed owns and has title of the painting. However, there are consequences if the work is stolen or if the consignor does not have ownership

When a collector consigns a piece of art, he or she "entrusts" the dealer with the ownership and gives the dealer the right to pass ownership to the dealer's buyers. Even if the dealer fails to pay the consignor, it does not affect the passage of ownership to the buyer. In such occurrences, the consignor has little recourse against the buyer unless the consignor can demonstrate collusion between the seller and buyer.

In the case of stolen art, no title can be transferred, and if a stolen painting is sold, the original owner retains ownership and has recourse against the seller and the buyer. The owner is entitled to have the piece returned without any compensation to the buyer. The only recourse for the buyer is against the dealer for breach of title warranty.

Art buyers can protect themselves against such a breach of warranty by buying art title insurance which protects in the same way as home title insurance. Depending on the piece, the cost of art title insurance runs between 2% to 5%. Although it is rarely negotiated on the sales contract, the cost of the insurance can be passed on to the dealer.

The best protection against authenticity and title problems is a strong provenance for the artwork. Provenance is the historical documentation of the painting which includes sales records, participated exhibitions and other relevant information. If such provenance exists, it should be noted on the sales contract so if the provenance turns out to be faulty, the dealer, not the buyer, suffers the repercussions.

To avoid authenticity and title problems with art acquisitions, the buyer should deal only with dealers with strong reputations, and who have demonstrated by their actions a real concern for the welfare of their clients. Major auction houses are particularly sensitive to retaining positive relationships with their clients. Also, the auction houses include in their consignment agreements the right of rescission, which allows the auction to cancel any sale if disputes arise. In this case, the art is returned to the seller who refunds the purchase price to the buyer. The right of rescission protects the buyer, but places a burden on the seller with the possibility that a future refund demand might be possible.

Selling art: consignment problems

When a collector consigns a piece of art to a dealer, he or she is trusting the dealer to sell the art, and to pay the collector for the sale. History has shown that this trust is often misplaced. Once the art is physically in possession of the dealer, the collector loses much of the control over the art regardless of protections in the consignment agreement. Selling art is always a challenge, and dealers will always claim they have a clientele of motivated buyers. It is not uncommon for a piece of art to lay dormant on the dealer's showroom for a year. If the dealer has the buyers he claims, a piece should sell in a few months if not weeks. For the seller, it makes no sense to sign a consignment agreement that gives the dealer exclusive selling rights for more than six months. It is not a positive sign when dealer demands exclusive consignment rights for a year.

If the work is a desirable piece, consigning it to an auction is usually the preferable alternative. Sales commissions at auction houses are usually half that charged by dealers and galleries. Although there are no guarantees that the work will sell at auction, the collector has immediate information instead of vague promises.

Some artist's works that have a very limited range of appeal with only a few dealers making a market for the artist. In such situations, the collector may have no choice but to consign with such dealers. Most dealers maintain a website showing their inventory of artists' works. Before shipping work to the dealer, the collector should monitor the site to evaluate the level of activity for the specific artist's works. If nothing moves in six months, it is not a good indication the dealer has an active client base for that artist.

Collectors face an even a worse risk when consigning art to the dealer — the risk the dealer fails to pay the collector. Failure in the art business is high, and even dealers who are fundamentally honest may be delinquent in paying collectors and artists for sold paintings. Some more notorious dealers enter into agreements without any intention of honoring them. In a marketplace that is basically unregulated, the importance of trust cannot be overestimated.

Once a piece is consigned to a dealer, the collector loses much of the control over the piece. Consigned art becomes a part of the dealer's inventory, and that inventory is subject to claim by any creditor. This includes the local taxing authorities, the federal government, the landlord and even other consignors. There is little in a dealer's consignment agreement that protects the consignor. There are some provisions in the consignment agreement that can afford some protection such as filing a UCC-1 financing statement which gives notice to subsequent creditors, but few dealers are willing to provide such protections. Regardless, of the verbiage in the consignment agreement, courts tend to favor the claims of the creditor over those of the consignor.

These same consignment risks also apply to auction houses, but such risks are minimal for the major houses, and only apply to the smaller auction houses which do not possess the financial resources of the larger houses. There is an additional risk for auction houses when successful bidders fail to pay for work. Auction houses handle this scenario differently. Most simply rescind the sale and return the painting to the consignor. Most will also offer to include the panting in the next auction without charging the consignor for auxiliary fees such as catalog and other marketing items. For important clients, the larger auction houses may simply pay the consignor and place the work into their own inventory.

In an unregulated market such as art, even the most judicious collector-investor will encounter the potential for problems. There are legal remedies, but they are costly and not always effective. To avoid these problems, the collector is advised to deal only with trustworthy individuals and companies. Unfortunately, identifying these individuals and companies is not always obvious.

Art consultants and advisers

Art adviser and *art consultant* are fairly interchangeable titles. Art consultant refers most frequently to a company or individual providing services for one-time projects, especially corporate projects whereas art adviser implies a continuing relationship. Art adviser is probably the more accurate term to describe a person who advises an individual art investor.

Art investors are usually fairly knowledgeable in art. However, when making significant investments in art, many art investors avail themselves of the services of an art adviser. Although the art adviser commission on an acquisition may increase the cost of the acquisition an additional 10%, the art adviser may negotiate a significant discount or may prevent the investor from making an ill-advised purchase.

The primary reason to engage an art adviser is to acquire desirable investment grade art at cost-effective prices. Investment grade art is in short supply, especially the work of historically significant artists. Many of these pieces may come from collections that will never be available on the open market. Private art sales imply sales that are not open to the public. Having an art adviser who has insider connections can allow a collector an opportunity to secure work that would never be available to the investor alone.

Besides assistance in the acquisition of the art, advisers also can assist the investor in selling the art. A connected adviser not only knows who is selling art, but also who is buying art. Often a private sale to an eager buyer can yield a net higher price than would have been achieved at an auction. When an auction is the preferable sales option, the art adviser can recommend the most appropriate auction at the most opportune time.

Art advisers can also offer a wide range of other services besides the actual buying and selling of art. A large art collection can involve a great deal of logistic activity especially when the investor is an active buyer and seller. Collectors also receive frequent requests to loan work to museums. Exposing a painting in the right museum exhibition can have expansive effect on the value of the art. The art adviser cannot only advise the collector on exhibition opportunities, but also on handling the administrative and logistic work that would be involved.

Some art advisers are called upon to oversee the installation of the collection in the home or in a corporate setting. Installations can be a complicated activity. Installing a two-ton monumental bronze can be a major undertaking.

Most art advisers insist that perhaps their most important role is helping to educate the client regarding the intricacies of the art market. This function is frequently more social than educational as the adviser will introduce the collector to galleries, dealers and the artists themselves. For many collectors, this social component may be the most important, so the art adviser must not only have art smarts, but also possess strong social skills.

Art advisers are not to be confused with financial advisers. Most advisers come out of art-related businesses, but they usually do not possess the acumen to advise the client on legal and financial matters. Thus, the investor-collector is probably wise to supplement his art advisory team with a tax attorney and accountant specializing in art.

Before recruiting an art adviser, the collector should consider the functions that are required. Some advisers are only interested in the acquisition and sale of art and bill their clients a percentage of the sale or purchase. If the collector was looking for someone to help maintain their collection, such an adviser would not serve that function. There are collectors who have already established themselves as influential players in the art market, and have little need for social introductions. Whereas for many collectors, such a service would be invaluable.

Most collector-investors have some idea of the kind of art they wish to acquire. Art advisers usually have particular areas of expertise. A collector who intends to invest in historically traditional work should recruit an art adviser who has expertise in that field. Conversely, if the collector was interested in modern contemporary work of living artists, an advisor who was connected with this community would be the best choice. The collector should quiz the potential adviser on some of the artists the collector may be interested, and evaluate the adviser's knowledge of these artists. This is particularly important for a collector who is collecting contemporary work. It makes no sense to recruit an adviser who has less knowledge than the collector.

When interviewing adviser prospects, the collector should be very clear in understanding what services they require from an adviser and to make those requirements clear in the interview. For once the adviser agreements have concluded, it is an uncomfortable process in breaking them.

In the art community, there are many people who promote themselves as art advisers or art consultants. Working six months in a gallery does not qualify a person as an art adviser. A crucial undertaking for the art investor is to find an art adviser who is highly connected in the art community. These individuals can't be found in the yellow pages so the investor-collector will have to do some research. This may begin by querying friends who have significant collections. They may have art advisers they employ. But friends may reluctant to give up the name of their art adviser since conflicts of interest could arise. Gallery owners and managers are a second possibility, but recommendations from galleries may be biased and lean to advisers with whom they do business. As was noted earlier, purchasing art at galleries is the least cost-effective way to purchase art.

After a list of potential advisers has been established, the collector should allocate sufficient time to interview each. Most advisers also deal in art, which will bias them toward artists whom they specialize and also have inventory. Separating the dealer from the true adviser is often difficult to assess, but an individual who discloses that he or she currently holds some desirable pieces may indicate they would be more interested in selling from their inventory. An informative question to ask is for the individual to discuss recent acquisitions he or she has facilitated. The quality of these pieces will indicate much about his or her influence in the art community. The interviewer may also ask for a list of the adviser's current clients and whether they can be contacted. Advisers who are reluctant to provide the list could indicate some problems with their business. Finally, since the collector will be spending much time with the adviser, it is important that there is a friendly rapport.

Art adviser compensation depends primarily on the kind and amount of work expected of the adviser. If the collector requires consultation services, the compensation may be per-hour basis, which could be about $100 hour, but this varies greatly on the experience of the adviser. There may also be a retainer fee that is also subject to negotiation.

Compensation may also be based on a percentage of the sales or purchase price. Generally that figure is about 10% but may be lower for art over $100,000. If art is purchased through a gallery, the gallery may provide the adviser a discount of usually about 10%. How such discounts are handled between the client and the adviser should be clearly outlined in the client-adviser contract.

For very large collections, the art adviser position may require full-time effort, and the compensation is much like employment contract. Like an employment contract, it should specify the number of hours that are expected to be devoted to the position. Employment benefits such as health insurance and vacation are usually not included. Compensation in these cases depend the number of hours that the adviser is expected to devote to the client. For a full-time adviser, the compensation could exceed $100,000.

To avoid the potential of future disagreements, the client-adviser contract needs to fully define the expected functions and obligations of the adviser with compensation for these functions. For instance, if the client requests the adviser to attend an art opening at a nearby gallery should those hours be billed and at what rate? Conversely, the adviser might invite the client to an opening. So would the client be billed in this situation? The client-adviser agreement should have these possibilities outline in the agreement. But no matter, how defined the agreement, there will always be occasions which involve activities that are not specified in the agreement. So the agreement should include some verbiage in the agreement stating that the adviser would be obligated to get the client's approval for any expense not specified in the agreement.

The art adviser represents an additional cost to the investor-collector, so the goal of the investor is to find and contract with an adviser who will save the collector money. Good advisers are the ones who save the investor more money than they cost, and these are the ones who are most difficult to find.

Other art investments

Art investment opportunities other than directly purchasing art are few. Art investment funds offer a diversified way to invest in a portfolio of art, but they are only available to very high income investors. Because the art market is generally unregulated, funds cannot market themselves to the general public, but only to "accredited investors." The Securities Exchange Commission defines the accredited investor as one with a net worth of at least $1 million and incomes of at least $200 thousand. In the era of the super-rich these wealth criteria are fairly modest, but it does restrict the art funds from marketing to the general public.

The art funds operate much like hedge funds in that they are organized as a LLC (Limited Liability Company) with a restricted number of investors, who are the limited partners. The funds are managed by the general partners. The general partners usually have some level of art market sophistication, but they also employ art advisers to assist in the investment decisions. Limited partner investments usually range from $100,000 to a $1 million. The number of partners may be as few fifty or as high as a few hundred. Investors are restricted in their prerogatives to withdraw from a fund. Time restrictions for withdrawal may be from one year to an indefinite period when the fund is liquidated. The compensation for the general partners differs for each funds. Usually it includes a management fee with some percentage of profits from liquidated art.

Many of the funds outline the artistic scope of the assets. For instance, the fund may only invest in contemporary art from a specific period, and may even specify the artists in which they will invest.

The number art funds is fairly small, probably under 100 with many of them organized in China. Because the funds are private and don't have to disclose their portfolios, it is difficult to evaluate their performance until the funds are liquidated. Some funds may not liquidate any art for many years, so there is no year-to-year accounting. Information provided to partner investors will be based on some assessment of the portfolio, but such assessments are always subjective. Every piece of art is unique and what that piece of art may fetch on the open market is subject to great variability.

Art funds present significant advantages and disadvantages for the investor. Primarily, it allows the investor the opportunity to diversify their assets. Not only is diversity added to the portfolio of financial assets, but also diversity to the portfolio of art assets.

One advantage of art funds is the art investor not only shares in a portfolio of art, but also access to services of a professional art adviser. For the private art collector-investor, acquisition and sales cost can be significant. Purchasing art through an auction can add 25% or more to the purchase while that figure may be twice that at a gallery. Most art funds secure a large percentage of their art through dealers and private sales where acquisition fees are much less that other acquisition options. Like a hedge fund, the ability of the managers of the fund are paramount to its success. However, unlike a mutual fund where performance is documented, the abilities of art fund managers are not so manifest.

As an investment vehicle art funds have not enjoyed great popularity. The steep initial investment precludes all but a few investor-collectors. Lack of transparency is another problem. Although the fund may provide a complete portfolio accounting, few art fund investors are privy to a visual inspection of the portfolio. Even if such an inspection were possible, the portfolio collection will have some dispersion. Some work may be on loan to museums and occasionally even to other investors in the fund.

Regardless of the sophistication of the general partners and their advisers, there always a risk of authenticity problems with the works. The same risks apply to the individual collector, but the individual can evaluate his or her own level of potential risk when acquiring work. The art fund investor depends on the fund manager's discretion in their acquisition policies and their attitude toward acceptable risk.

One of the greatest drawbacks for art funds is their lack of liquidity. In most cases, the investor is locked into the fund for a considerable time and cannot withdraw from the fund regardless of the circumstances. Individual collectors can always consign the work for auction and may even receive a money advance from the auction, especially for a desirable work. Banks will also make loans with art serving as the collateral. Recently, there has been the emergence of financial institutions specializing in art loans.

For many investor-collectors, the joy of possession is important factor in the acquisition of art. Although some art funds will loan work to their investors, it does not come with the same joy of ownership. Similarly, most investor-collectors enjoy the process of collecting art, especially the social opportunities that are afforded.

Because art funds are not required to publicly disclose their performance, it is impossible to evaluate the performance of such funds. There is also little anecdotal chatter on these funds, and that which is heard tends to be negative. A fund originating from a desirable private collection might have real potential investment potential, but as an investment, it would appear that self-acquisition of investment grade art has significant advantages over the art fund shares.

The fact that art funds have shown limited investment appeal is probably an indictment in itself. There have been a few attempts to create art investment vehicles that could be marketed to the general public, but the unregulated environment of art has restricted their development. It is doubtful that such funds will be developed in the immediate future.

Most of the major auction houses are privately owned with Sotheby's as the only exception. As the only publicly traded auction house, Sotheby's is the major art-related stock option for investors. The extreme competition with other auction houses for ever-decreasing high-grade investment art has been severe, constricting profit margins. The auction houses have attempted to raise commission rates to compensate for the lower profit margins. This has led to increased level of private sales which also has had a depressing effect on their revenue and profit.

A few arts related internet companies, such as ArtNet have gone public, but the majority operate as privately held companies. These companies have struggled to generate profits, but may deserve continued attention as they evolve in their business model.

How the internet has changed the art market

The internet has radically changed the art market. It has become much more transparent and competitive. For the savvy collector, it has brought down the price of art, and for galleries and dealers, it has significantly reduced their profit margins. Dealers, who in the past may have made 50% profit on their deals, now feel fortunate if they can make 20%.

The internet has caused other significant art market changes. The most important of these is the availability of price information. Virtually every painting that is sold at auction is recorded by a growing number of internet auction reporting sites. Initially, the fees to access these sites were fairly expensive, but competition has driven prices down. So when a potential seller brings a piece of art to a dealer, he or she has probably conducted some research on the internet, and has some idea of the value of the piece. Conversely, when a dealer attempts to sell an artwork, potential buyers have also done their homework and have some idea of its value.

Not only is it effortless to discover recent prices for work, but the images for these pieces are also available. This means there are far fewer "fresh" paintings that come to market. Before the internet, a dealer could purchase a work at a secondary auction and within a short time resell the piece at a major auction for significant profit. Bidders at the major auction now know exactly how much the piece sold for at the earlier auction. The dealer can still make a profit if he or she acquired undervalued work, but the purchase information certainly has a limiting price effect on subsequent sales. Dealers who have their own clientele can bypass auctions and save on auction commissions, but their clientele are also much more informed from their own internet research which has constricting influence on sale prices.

The internet has been a boon for old collectors who have seen the value of their collection increase significantly in value. New collectors have benefitted from smaller dealer markups, but they face greater competition and higher prices in the secondary market.

Expanding purchase options

The second factor that has greatly influenced the art market is the expanding number of options to purchase art. The development of internet auction technology has provided small auction houses with the ability to offer their consigned pieces to a national and international market. So in the past when their potential buyers consisted of the seventy-five bidders in their auction room, the auction house may have ten times that in internet bidders. This significantly increases the competition, and hence, the price for the work. This is good for the selling collector and the auction house, but not so good for the buyer and limits the dealer's opportunities. Because of the development of these technologies, new art auctions have emerged with art galleries and other arts-related enterprises moving into the auction industry to attempt to offset declining revenues in their core businesses.

The decline of galleries

Galleries have also experienced increasing financial pressure from the internet. Although the internet has provided galleries with new marketing and selling tools, it also has incubated new competitors. Many new online galleries have appeared offering art at prices significantly less than their brick and mortar counterparts.

Galleries with their high markups have never been an economical source of investment grade art. However, they did represent a fairly large sales segment of the auction buyers. Like private dealers, they have also been negatively impacted by the internet. Their margins have declined, and probably more significant, the availability of quality investment grade art has declined. Many of these galleries had relied on auction purchases for their inventory. Today, they are competing against more aggressive bidders in the form of savvy collectors and other galleries and dealers. Recently, a gallery owner friend closed her gallery after 30 years of operation. Her collectors were still buying work, but she could no longer attract new inventory.

For galleries, who sell contemporary and emerging artists work, the internet has also generated new competitors, primarily their own artists. Artists have discovered that the internet provided them with a new effective selling tool. Many of the hot-selling artists realized they could sell their own work online without giving the galleries a healthy chunk in commissions. There has also been an emergence of online selling sites where the artist can place their art for a much smaller commission than they would have to pay their galleries.

Internationalization

Art has always been a global market, but the evolution of the internet has accelerated the process. American collectors can now bid live online at galleries around the world. And with the rapid growth of Asian economies, new wealthy collectors have become active bidders at the major auctions in America. To accommodate these collectors, the major American auctions have opened offices and auctions in many major Asian cities.

In the 1950's and 60's, American art brokers used to travel to Europe and commission artists to create work that they would bring back to America and sell to many galleries as "fine European paintings." Most of the paintings were signed with fictitious names, but would still sell for a few thousand dollars. Today, collectors can bid in European auctions, and purchase paintings from fairly recognized artists for less than buyers paid fifty years ago for these generic imported paintings.

Over the last thirty years, we have seen the development of art factories. The first of these were in Europe, then Mexico and most recently in China and Russia. The quality of the work is mixed, but some of it is very good. In fact, some of the recreations of major artists' work may challenge the original work,

Most of these paintings are directed to the weekend "starving artists" shows offered at hotels where buyers can purchase a large oil painting for under $100. After purchasing a starving artist piece, it is highly unlikely these buyers will ever move up to the prices charged by fine art galleries. These inexpensive factory paintings fill as much space on collectors' walls as work sold in galleries.

Effect on art prices

So how has the internet affected art prices? Generally, the more competitive a market, the lower the price for the product. The internet has made the art market more competitive, and we have seen declining prices for some segments of the art market, primarily the lower priced contemporary and emerging art market.

However, for investment grade art the picture is different as prices have risen. Prices for major auction pieces have increased, especially for the highest grade investment art where the supply has declined while demand has risen. At auctions, greater competition, e.g., more buyers, means higher prices.

For the art investor who has already assembled a portfolio of investment grade art, the financial prospects are very positive. For the new art investor, the availability of prime pieces had diminished, and the cost to secure even secondary work will continue to climb. It would appear that as long the we don't see an international deflation, prices should continue to rise insuring future profits.

Speculating in art: the return of the patron

With the growth of the internet with its global dissemination of art information, there are few undiscovered significant works of art. Walking into a backwater antique store and finding hidden jewels is something of the past. Even that backwater antique store owner is connected to the internet. Certainly every few months, we hear of a masterpiece that was discovered in some attic, but these instances are rare and becoming rarer.

There is no question that the supply of high investment grade art is dwindling and will continue to increase in value. Yet, with acquisition costs high, the investor may have to hold the art for extended periods of time to generate any profit at all. For the work of major historic artists, there is little chance of declining prices. For the new art investor with fairly modest capital to invest, a portfolio of a few pieces from secondary artists may be the only possibility.

Although there may be only a few undiscovered works of the master artists, there is an overabundance of art of undiscovered artists. The real opportunities in art investment may be in the speculation in the art of today's emerging artists. The historical precedent for this goes back to the turn of the Nineteenth Century when a few savvy collectors saw the potential in the works of the Impressionist and post-Impressionist artists. More recently, the early paintings of the 1970's and 80's New York street artists such as Jean Michael Basquiat and Keith Haring now command millions at auction

Many of these collectors purchased the art for the love of the work, but they also saw themselves as patrons. Some patrons have had instrumental roles in the success of the artists they supported. One of the most famous is Peggy Guggenheim who supported the work of Jackson Pollock. Perhaps, the most astounding patrons of recent era were Dorothy and Herb Vogel who were middle class New York couple, who started collecting art in the late 1960's. Over five decades, the Vogels collected thousands of paintings, most of them from Minimalist artists such as Roy Lichtenstein and Richard Tuttle. In 1990 they donated the bulk of their collection to the National Museum. The value of the collection would probably fetch hundreds of millions if sold at auction today.

Although Vogels were constant visitors to New York's trendy and not so trendy galleries, they rarely purchased from galleries, but rather from the artists themselves. Buying directly from the artist is an essential characteristic of patrons. Not only does the patron enjoy the pleasure of interacting with the artist, but also saving the commissions and fees they would have had to spend with galleries and brokers. There is no question that dealing directly with the artist allowed them to accumulate their vast collection.

The Vogel experience serves as a lesson for all art investors and speculators: buying directly from the artist is always preferable to buying from dealers and galleries. The most obvious reason is that it is easier to negotiate price from the artist when there is not a forty or fifty percent commission involved. Some artists will refuse to sell directly to collectors, but the harsh realities of an art life, especially for emerging artists, makes it difficult to refuse potential sales. Many artists have ambivalent relationships with their galleries and feel that gallery commissions are not justified for what they receive from the galleries. Then, there are some artists who refuse to work with galleries and sell their own work. Regardless of the relationship between the artist and gallery, artists always sell out of their studio. Most of Picasso's greatest paintings never made it to a gallery.

Once a collector has established a good relationship with the artist, he or she may often have access to the artist's best work before the paintings leave the artist's studio. Artists have even been known to hold exclusive gatherings with collectors before shipping new work to galleries. Etta and Claribel Cone, Baltimore's famous collector sisters, would receive letters from Henri Matisse when he was need of quick cash.

In some cases the patron relationship can even be formalized where the collector agrees to purchase a certain number of paintings over a specified number of months. In a typical case, the collector would visit the artist's studio and purchase one painting. The relationship benefits both the artist and collector. The artist has a guaranteed income and the collector has the choice of the artist's best work. The patron realizes financial benefits of such relationships and a personal pleasure in supporting the artist's career and to connect with the artist on a personal level. Many artists, especially young ones, can experience self-doubts about their art and themselves. So having strong relationships with collectors who value them and their work not only helps to sustain them financially but also emotionally.

Collector-artist relationships usually begin with a visit to the artist's studio. Most artists welcome the opportunity to show off their work to potential collectors. Often, these visits may lead to an immediate purchase, but even without a purchase both the collector and the artist can find the interaction rewarding. Like any successful human relationship, it must be based on mutual respect. However, patronage can have a negative repercussion. The artist may become so dependent upon the collector that the artist's creative drive disappears and with it the quality of the work. For the patron, artist dependency can become extremely burdensome and difficult to sever.

As a financial decision, art speculation is extremely risky. Even for extremely gifted artists, success is elusive, and for the art speculator, rewards are rarely realized in the short-term. The time frame for art speculation is often measured in decades, not years. Even for the speculator with a educated and savvy eye for innovative art, the potential for success is minimal. If ten percent of a speculator's purchases pans out, it is a good result.

It is impossible to be successful as a passive collector. Like the Vogels and the Cones, the art speculator has to be obsessive about art and artists. Today's art collector-speculator has the advantage of being able to review thousands of the artists' work on the internet. But seeing the work digitally is not the same as seeing the work in person. So much of the time for the speculator involves visiting art galleries and art events. Since the essential objective is to deal directly with the artist, it is important to circulate where these opportunities present themselves.

For those living in middle-America, there are few opportunities for art speculation. The collector has to have the resources and the willingness to travel. The art capital of the world is still New York, but the collector will also have to attend the major art fairs and the art destination cities from Basel to Miami. Again, for the art speculator, no destination is too far to discover great talent.

Great talent does not necessarily translate into great art — or at least art that commands great economic value. Finding artists who will create art that will be significant fifty years from now is a real challenge. Looking at historical precedents, the art should appear revolutionary and new such as Impressionism in the 1870's and Pop art in the 1960's. There should be a movement associated with the work being advanced by a small but vocal proponents for the work. Finally, the collector should become very knowledgeable with the movement and its artists, and to identify the leading proponents of the style.

The mind-set of the art speculator is quite different from the pure art investor. First, the speculator should truly appreciate the artist and his or her work. Since it is a strong probability the art will never appreciate significantly, the speculator should enjoy living with the work and find some satisfaction in supporting artists' careers. Like the art they collect, the art speculator must be a visionary, and not afraid to trust the vision.

Final words: buyer beware

No other form of investment is more subject to fraud and deception than in the art business. Deceptive practices are perpetrated on the most savvy dealers and collectors, so the non-professional art investor has to exercise extreme caution in his or her art dealings. The deals that look too good to pass up are the deals that usually should be avoided.

Authenticity is a critical issue when purchasing art. Is the painting or sculpture what the seller claims it to be? The overriding determinant for the value of a piece of art is the artist who created it. When visiting exhibitions of historically significant artists I am always surprised to discover a few pieces that are technically deficient, and maybe even worse, downright boring. Nevertheless, even these paintings with their deficiencies may still fetch millions of dollars at auction. The value is in the signature.

Protecting yourself from subsequent issues of authenticity is not an easy matter. Buyers can purchase title insurance, but there is no insurance for authenticity except for the buyer's own due diligence.

One should deal only with dealers and galleries that have developed trustworthy reputations. Any hint of malfeasance should disqualify any dealer for business consideration. I have known more than a few victims of fraudulent deals who admitted there were red flags they ignored. Doing some dealer research is always recommended especially when dealing with a new dealer or broker. One doesn't need to hire a private detective, but can learn much simply by doing an internet search.

A few years ago, I became involved with an attractive woman who required appraisals for some secondary French Impressionist paintings. She needed the appraisals for a few potential clients of the work. She was very flattering which stroked my ego, but I found it to be a bit too flattering, so I decided to do a little research before taking on the project. My research uncovered that she had been arrested in Las Vegas for art fraud. This wasn't a total surprise, but what was the shocker was that she was really a he. I suggested that she might consider the services of another art appraiser. I have no doubt she succeeded.

Even for dealers we trust, precautions need to be taken. Most important is a sales contract which should explicitly describe the work with all of the physical dimensions as well as any other claims by the dealer on the piece and the artist. Many collectors place too much trust in the dealers with whom they are working, and take them at their word without getting those words on paper.

Perhaps, the best insurance is a complete provenance for the work. Newly discovered pieces found in a Paris basement should be eyed with a certain amount incredulity. Of course, provenance can also be forged, but there have been few reported cases where that has occurred. In most cases, provenance is a reliable source in determining artwork authenticity.

Art listed in a respected catalogue raisonné is also supportive in establishing the artwork's authenticity. A catalogue raisonné is a comprehensive, annotated listing of all the known artworks by the artist. It should be noted that some catalogs are more respected than others. Many artist's estates have developed lucrative businesses in certifying the artist's works. These estate certifications are far less accurate. In many cases, these certifiers are not always very competent in their judgments, and in many cases are more interested in income than reliability. The opposite can also be the case where estates with large inventories of the artist's work may reject true work to limit competitive pieces on the market.

Buying art from another collector presents many of the same cautions as buying from a dealer or gallery. There can be issues with authenticity, and even a greater danger is one of title. With a gallery or dealer, there is a fairly good possibility the seller secured the painting from a reputable source. With an individual, there is

Final Words: Bujyer Beward

far less certainty. The seller may be a drug addict who absconded with the art from the family home. On a larger scale, there is the art that was confiscated from Jewish collectors in Nazi Germany. Now, three quarters of a century later, these paintings are being returned to the rightful heirs without any compensation to the current owners even though the paintings may have been purchased in good faith without knowledge of their history. This is another argument for insisting on provenance.

Problems with authenticity are compounded when the purchase is from another individual. The legal transaction protections that are included with a dealer purchase do not fully apply to transaction between individuals. With dealers, the presumption is that their expertise exposes them to legal remedies if authenticity comes into question. With individual collectors, there is no such presumption and therefore limited protections.

Selling and buying art at auction can also be subject to insider manipulation. Auction bidders can collude by either bidding prices up or conversely refraining from bidding against other colluders. Auction manipulation can occur at all auctions, but it is most prevalent at the smaller regional auctions, especially auctions without national internet capability. This capability has provided some protection against collusion, but it still can occur. The best defense for the collector is to attend the auction to get a sense whether collusion is occurring.

The problem with the online auctions is that the potential buyer cannot inspect the work, and must rely on the auction house for an accurate description of the piece. It is a safe practice to never buy a piece without seeing it in person. Most galleries will send a piece to recognized collectors on approval but that is not the case for auctions. Buying a piece online from another collector or directly from the artist is also a risky proposition unless you have developed a previous relationship with the seller.

Authenticity is an issue with all mediums of art, but reproductive art such as lithographs and etchings is rife with counterfeits. In my appraisal practice, certain artist's works seem particularly susceptible. The three artists I encounter the most problems are Picasso, Salvador Dali and Marc Chagall. It is reported that Dali signed 10,000 blank sheets before he died. Most serious collectors avoid reproductive art because of the counterfeit issue plus reproductions rarely increase in value at the same rate as originals.

As a gallery owner I have had thousands of discussions regarding artists and their work, and only in a handful of instances did the collector inquire about the future financial prospects of the artist's works. I know some galleries this is a major part of their sales pitch. I think it is virtually impossible to project the financial future for any artist's work, and I am suspicious of those who believe they can portend how an artist will be viewed fifty years from now. Given the unlikelihood of any contemporary artist becoming historically significant, the collector should select art that provides them with aesthetic pleasure for they will be sharing space in the foreseeable future.

Beware:
"How do you make a small fortune in art?"
"You start with a large one."

Appendix 1
Art auction terms

Appraisal	A formal analysis of the value of an artwork usually resulting in a written document used for tax and insurance purposes.
As Is	The property is sold with all existing faults and imperfections and buyer loses most recourse against the auction or seller.
Attribution	The artist assignation of a piece of art. If an attributed piece of art is not authenticated, it may carry the description "attributed to."
Auctioneer	The individual who presides over the auction, initiating the sale of a lot by describing the item and starting the bidding
Authentication	Documented proof or expert opinion confirming the authenticity of an item of art.
Authenticity	The art is genuine and produced by the artist to whom it is attributed.
Authorship	Used in auction catalogs to identify the creator of an artwork.
Bid	A price offered by an individual when he/she want to buy a lot.
Bid Increment	The amount by which the auctioneer increases the bidding.
Bought-In	If a lot does not receive any bids or does not meet the reserve price, the lot is returned to consignor, and the term "brought in" will be listed.
Buy-in fees	The fee the consignor must pay when a lot does not sell. Ranges from 3-6%.
Buyer's premium	An additional amount added to the hammer price of a paid lot. The commission charged to the buyer.

Catalogue	After items are collected for a sale, a catalogue is published which lists the lots in the auction.
Commission	The fee the consignor and buyer must pay the auctioneer when the auction sells an artwork.
Condition report	A written description of the condition of a work, prepared by the auction house.
Conditions of business	Special conditions under which an item is offered for sale. These conditions effect the rights of buyer.
Consignor	An individual who consigns work to an auction house for sale.
Consignment agreement	An agreement between the auction and the consignor outlining the rights of each.
Designation	A generic description of the consignor as opposed to actual name.
Estimate	The price range an artwork is expected to sell at an auction.
Fair market value	Is the price that the art would sell for on the open market between a willing buyer and a willing seller, with neither being required to act and both have reasonable knowledge of the relevant facts.
Guarantee	Some amount the auction house has offered the consignor whether the item sells or not.
Hammer price	The winning bid for a lot at an auction (named after the action of the auctioneer using his/her hammer to signal the end of bidding). The hammer price is included in the Price List and usually does not include the Buyer's Premium.
Insurance value	Is the amount it would cost to replace an item with one of similar and like quality purchased in the most appropriate marketplace within a limited amount of time. Also called replacement value.

Insurance fee	The fee paid to an auction house to insure a consigned lot.
Knocked down	An auction house term for the hammer coming down and ending the bidding, as in, "The lot was knocked down at $1 million."
Lot	An individual object or group of objects for sale in an auction. Auction catalogs are arranged by lot number.
Paddle	An object displaying the number assigned to a bidder when he or she registers at the auction.
Pass/unsold	Terms used by the auctioneer when an item fails to reach its reserve at auction.
Price list	After a sale is completed, a list of final sale prices for each lot is recorded.
Price realized	The complete price a buyer pays for an item. Price realized includes the hammer price, the buyer's premium, and any additional fees or taxes.
Provenance	Documentation providing the history of the ownership of a specific artwork.
Rescission rights	The right of the auction to rescind a sale and returning the item to the seller and money to the buyer.
Replacement value	Is the amount it would cost to replace an item with one of similar and like quality purchased in the most appropriate marketplace within a limited amount of time. Also called insurance value.
Resale rights	Royalties that may be paid to living arts for resale of their work. These fees are charged to the buyer of the work.
Reserve price	The minimum selling price for an artwork agreed upon by the consignor and the auction house.

Appendix 2
Informative Websites

Appraising Art www.appraisingart.com	Everything a collector needs to know about art appraisals and appraisers
Art Appraisers of America www.artappraisersofamerica.com	A comprehensive list of art appraisers by state, city and specialty.
Art Auction Primer www.artauctionprimer.com	Selling your art at an auction can be a complicated matter. Site offers information on every facet of sales as well as a comprehensive list of auction terms.
Art Auctions of America www.artauctionsofamerica.com	A comprehensive list of art auctions by state, city. Plus detailed information on how to select an auction to sell and buy work.
Collecting Art www.collectingart.net	Information for the art collector including recent art trends.
Investing in Art www.investinginart.net	Site for collectors who are seeking to realize financial gains from their art portfolio.
AUCTION HOUSES	
Christie's www.christies.com	A major American international auction house with locations worldwide.
Sotheby's www.sothebys.com	The other major American auction with international offices.
Bonhams www.bonhams.com	A third major international auction house but without the prestige of the top two.
ArtNet www.artnet.com	The first major online auction house offering American and European art. One of the few publicly traded auction sites
ArtSpace www.artspace.com	A second major online auction house with both American and European art.

Other Innovative Books
by RL Foster

To the Artist in Search of a Gallery (2014)
Selling Your Own Art (2016)

Available

WWW. INNOVATIVEBOOKS.NET

COVER

Study for The Chahut

by *Georges Seurat*

www.ingramcontent.com/pod-product-compliance
Lightning Source LLC
Chambersburg PA
CBHW020452220526
45464CB00002B/964